The Power of Love

for Uncomplicated Christians

by Fr. Emile Brière

MADONNA HOUSE | PUBLICATIONS

Combermere, Ontario | Canada   K0J 1L0

Cover Design: Marilyn Reaves

Nihil Obstat: Rev. Robert D. Pelton

Imprimatur:

> J.R. Windle
>
> +Bishop of Pembroke
>
> May 1990

The Nihil Obstat and Imprimatur are a declaration that a book or pamphlet is considered to be free from doctrinal or moral error. It is not implied that those who have granted the Nihil Obstat and Imprimatur agree with the contents, opinions or statements expressed.

Canadian Cataloguing in Publication Data

Brière, Emile
The power of love

First published as: For Uncomplicated Christians.
Boston: St. Paul Editions, 1973.
ISBN 0-921440-17-0

1. Love – Religious aspects – Christianity.
2. Christian life. I. Title II. Title: For Uncomplicated Christians.

BV4639.B79 1990   248.4   C90-090273-6

MADONNA HOUSE   PUBLICATIONS

Combermere, Ontario   Canada   K0J 1L0

PRINTED IN CANADA

CONTENTS

Foreword

"The entrance of your words gives light; it gives understanding to the simple" (Ps 119:130).

When I first met Father Emile Brière, he had been ordained not quite 16 years. He was still a young priest, though I didn't realize it because he was so evidently seasoned in faith, in wisdom, in suffering, and above all in love.

At that time Father Brière had just begun his life within the Madonna House Apostolate. Like the other priests who founded the priests' branch of Madonna House, he had lived his public ministry first, and then followed the Lord's call to Combermere in order to enter Nazareth. Only six months out of my teens and at the very moment of coming into the Church, I had no idea what Christ was asking of these priests. Now, 34 years later, as Father Brière prepares to celebrate his golden anniversary of priesthood, I do.

To enter Nazareth means to surrender completely to the power of Christ's love. Father Brière had already been living that surrender but, within Madonna House, Christ's Mother — with the special help of Catherine Doherty — focused it in the very center of his heart. There, the Holy Spirit would make it as total as Our Lady's surrender and unite it completely with that of Christ to the Father.

During these three and a half decades, one could

have seen an extremely busy Father Brière – always serving Catherine and Eddie, Father Callahan and the other priests, dozens of spiritual directees and countless others, teaching, listening, praying, and of course being crucified and raised up again. One might *not* have seen a gifted priest being transformed by the glory of the cross into a true icon of Christ.

Father Brière's "reflections on the power of love," then, are more than shrewd spiritual advice. His words give "understanding to the simple'" because the Incarnate Word has never ceased making Father Brière's life his own.

It is my privilege to say that Father Brière and I have been friends together as the Lord has worked with both of us. May his reflections on this work of love enlighten and console you as his words and his life have enlightened and consoled me.

> Father Robert D. Pelton
> Madonna House
> Easter, 1990

Introduction

The power of love that I write about is the power of God's love, the Lord's own love vitalizing a human heart, filling the Christian's heart, flowing to others from that redeemed heart. "The love of God has been poured into our hearts by the Holy Spirit which has been given to us," writes St. Paul. And St. John tells us that he is talking not so much about our love for God but about God's love for us.

For truly we have no love of our own. We are creatures. We have received all that we have. Of ourselves we have nothing and can do nothing. We are empty, dry, hollow, as an empty shell, as a dry well. No, of ourselves we have no love. It is a dreadful mistake to think that we have anything of our own to give anyone else. What can we give God except our emptiness, our misery, our sinfulness? To be filled, to be healed, to be forgiven, this is our task.

Passionately does the Lord desire to forgive all of our sins, to heal all of our wounds and to fill our whole being with His life and His love. Passionately does He love us, does He want us to know His love, to appreciate His love, to rest in His love, to live in His love, to be strengthened by His love. This world He gave us throbs with His love, and every human being is made in the image of the God who is love. Every one of us has an immense capacity for love — to be loved and to return love.

Yet the Lord's love means so little to our world! Who is thrilled by it, filled by it? Who stops, in the silence of his heart, to ponder over it? Who looks at a crucifix and says, "This was for me. I have been forgiven. See how much He loves me"? The Lord has few friends and fewer lovers. He wants you to know of His love for you. He waits upon your love. He has made you for love. Why are we so indifferent to Christ's love? Why are we so unmoved by the sight of His pain? Why are we so callous?

There may be many reasons. Pride, for instance, whose other name is ignorance. We want to be self-sufficient, independent, fulfilling our own needs ourselves. We refuse to acknowledge our poverty, our immense need for the love of God and of others. We refuse to live in reality, to see the obvious, and that is utter folly. Full of self-importance, we like to parade our puny ideas, our little accomplishments, our trivial joys and petty sorrows. We talk much, and the sound of our voices drowns out the strong beating of God's heart pounding at our ears.

Another reason may be that we really don't believe in love. We don't believe that it is possible to be loved and to love. We may have been hurt in the past or disappointed and disillusioned. We may have become sour, withdrawn from life and so from love. And yet, when we question our heart in the silence of the night, when we ask ourselves in a moment of sincerity, "What do I really want?" the answer comes back loud and clear, "I want to be loved, I want to live, I want to love."

Still a third reason why we may be indifferent to God's love is perhaps that we are afraid of love. Ashamed of our weaknesses, we don't want to be known lest we be rejected. We believe that God knows us as we are, but we don't quite believe that anyone can know us that well and still love and forgive us! We're afraid of commitments, of involvements. When one is loved, then one must respond, and that response means the gift of oneself, the loss of self. We fear that loss. It is a shattering experience for a mere creature to discover that God is love. The immense joy that suffuses the soul is quickly followed by fear—fear of illusion, fear of losing oneself, fear of mystery. A new dimension has entered one's life and nothing is quite the way it was before.

People and things have acquired a new beauty and goodness which serves only to add to one's hunger for God. One must love others and serve them quietly—without dramatics—and wait. One must be wary also of the enemy who will seek every opportunity to distress and confuse. He is vanquished by the simple means of trust in God, prayer, and fasting.

We are made for love. To be loved and to love is our destiny. Our greatness is to be able to love Another and to give oneself to Him and to others, thus preparing ourselves for the full life of heaven, where each belongs to each without fears, reservations, or limitations. There the beauty and goodness of God and of others will literally "take us out of ourselves" in an enduring and growing ecstasy of joy. *Perfect love casts out all fears.* God's love is perfect. Open your heart to it and all your fears will quickly and definitely disappear. Let us live today in the gentle power of God's love.

Do I
Believe
in Christ's
Love?

Christ has come. He has suffered and died for us. He has resurrected. We have been forgiven and redeemed. We have been chosen to bring to others the Good News of God's love for man. Do we believe in His love? Do we live this message? Do we bring it to others?

If the Son of God became one of us, if He has given the last drop of His blood for all men, if He has chosen me as a witness to His love, then I must make a response, I must change my life, I must take Him seriously...because He is God! Do I believe in Christ's love for me? Has this faith penetrated into my heart and soul and changed my life? Or do I live as if Christ had not come, as if His sacrifice and triumph had little to do with daily living? Am I indifferent to His great love?

He gave all for me. What do I think of that? What do I give Him? He chose me, He sent me forth to be an instrument of His love. He loves me so much

1

that He wants me to share in His work. By my love, by my trust and faith, He gives me the power to bring others to Himself. Do I realize that this immense and glorious power has been given to me? Or am I too lazy to be concerned about God's gifts, too cold-hearted to care about His pain, too self-centered to give much thought to the salvation of others?

Surely these are questions which will disturb us when we come to die — not so much our sins, as our omissions, our coldness, our lack of love, our indifference to the infinite love by which we were redeemed. It is better to face them now, squarely and clearly, while there is still time.

We have been bought at a great price. The Lord gave Himself, all of Himself, for us. How precious we are! How great He has made us! How great does He want all men to become! Sons of God, who live with His own life, who love with His own love. Despite our weaknesses, despite our misery and our failings, our hearts beat in rhythm with the merciful love of God, unless, of course, we expel Him from our lives. At baptism He came to us, Father, Son, and Holy Spirit. He came to stay, His creative power constantly at work, shaping, purifying, transforming. How great we are, united so intimately with God! Holiness, Power, Love, Life has sought us out and possessed us!

We have been bought at a great price. Therefore, we are great. Christ's pain has not been in vain. It has produced immense fruits, for He is God, and who shall estimate the value of the pain of God? We must appreciate who we are.

Who am I, really? I am the beloved of God. For *me* the mighty Creator of all things suffered torture, let Himself be humiliated, gave all of His blood, even to the last drop. For me — not just for mankind in general. Do I need more proof of His love, of my own greatness, of my power? For power He has given me to let others know of His great love for them also, to bring them to Him to be raised from the dead, to be transformed, to be united with Him.

Let us not fail His love and His trust. Having appreciated ever more deeply our own transformation and His love for us, let us bring others to Him. May the fire of zeal ignite in our hearts and burst forth ever stronger. Men, beloved of God, wait for us to greet them; they wait for our love.

Every Christian is called to be a missionary, a living embodiment of God's love in the world. Every Christian is well equipped for that task. Let each of us see that. Let each of us believe in what he has become, in what he can become. It isn't what we do that matters, but what we are. Good fruits come from good trees. Love flows from a loving person.

Such is our privilege and our task — and our power. Christ's love waits to be distributed to all men. He has paid the terrible price. He waits for us to pass on to others what He has so lavishly given to us.

"But what can I do?" you may ask. Believe in the love which is in you, and love today. Forget yourself. Be concerned about the needs of the person next to you. Be of service to that person. Each time you do, this, you die. Each time you die to your own selfishness by those little services rendered to others, you resurrect with Christ, and His love fills your world.

It's as simple as that.

You Can
Love
Right Now

A few years ago, in those dark days when the Communists were trying to incriminate Cardinal Wyszynski, primate of Poland, three girls belonging to a secular institute were arrested and thrown into prison. The comrades knew of the Cardinal's personal interest in this institute because as a priest he had participated actively in its foundation. They hoped that under pressure the girls would break down and "reveal" crimes committed by the Cardinal. Fortified by this "evidence," they could then proceed to bring the influential Cardinal to trial, condemn him, and remove him without incurring popular protest.

But their little diabolical plan failed. It failed because these girls loved. For weeks on end they were awakened in the middle of the night and dragged from their cells to the blinding lights of the interrogation room. There a woman party member subjected them to the vilest, most grueling and abject scrutiny imaginable.

Night after night their answers and their silence filled the room with peace and with love. They had determined they would love this woman. They prayed all day to be faithful to their heroic resolution. And one night, the inevitable happened. Their tormentor broke down. She told them to go, they were free. The girls rushed to her, surrounded her, embraced her, told her that each day until their death they would pray for her. Once again love, the love which is *caritas*, had overcome hatred and cruelty, and foiled the cunning of pride.

Your life too can be redemptive, if you fill it daily with its full measure of love, following the example of Jesus, Mary, and Joseph in their humble home at Nazareth.

And redemption is needed. Love is sadly needed in this loveless world. Many people say: "Things aren't too bad. There is much good in the world, in our cities, towns, and villages. Why not look on the bright side of things?" They resent any criticism of their communities, any pointing out of deficiencies, failings and sinfulness. It disturbs their false peace of soul. No one particularly wants to accept responsibility for religious indifference and social injustice. No one likes to be shown society's wounds and the neighbor's needs. It interferes with the pursuit of one's own "happiness." It places a burden upon the soul—the burden of the cross.

The evil is this: that Love is unloved; that men in making the practical decisions of daily life do not believe in God; that they treat one another as if they were not actual or potential members of the Body of Christ; that the "friends" of God fear Him much more than they love Him; that selfishness and greed and pride and envy and lust and hatred—frequently coated with a veneer of respectability, of religiosity

—still rule in many places. Witness unemployment, group tensions, adultery, juvenile delinquency, loveless families, and the immorality of much advertising.

Behind every social and individual problem we find the same cause: an absence of *caritas*, of strong, tender, enlightened love. The solution is clear. The solution is to love. And love will find a way. True enough, specialists are needed to assess and solve our problems as they arise: economists, politicians, psychiatrists, educators, theologians, and philosophers. But their solutions are sterile without love. It is love alone that makes them fruitful.

As a Christian begins to view his environment with the eyes of Christ, as he begins to assess it in the light of the Gospel, as he begins to be aware of his responsibility in the daily, relentless and unending struggle for the hearts and minds of men, he is bound to ask the question: "But what can *I* do? I am small, unimportant, uneducated. What can *I* do?"

Christ, our Lady, all the saints answer: "You can love. You can love right now. You can observe the two great commandments this minute. Thus you can become a saint and redeem your world."

Education, work, social standing, personal talents of themselves are unimportant. They are nothing but means whereby love serves, love expresses itself. Witness the humble home of Nazareth. Here Redemption was cradled and grew. Each day in Nazareth was full, important, different. Each day perfect adoration and praise went up to the Father. At every minute the world was being saved.

To be a Christian is to be another Christ, another adorer of the Father, another redeemer of men, another lover. A Christian family is another Holy Family where a father sanctifies the world by repeat-

ing the simple gestures of Jesus and Joseph, where a
mother redeems and gives praise by repeating the
simple gestures of Mary with a full heart. It is good
to call at the little house of Nazareth, to sit there
quietly and learn all we have to know, to be, and
to do in life.

How generous the Lord of love, that He has
made the greatest holiness accessible to everyone!
How lavish His daily gifts to His little ones, to His
little uncomplicated ones who daily say *fiat* in
their hearts, who believe that He is love, who trust
His love and His power daily, and who love daily.
To these He reveals His secrets and gives His greatest
gift: His cross—the greatest gift of the God of love.

Anybody can love. Anybody. Right now!

Nothing
To Lose
But Our
Fears

The needs of men, the needs of the Church are so immense that a veritable army of apostles are urgently required. Apostles of all kinds are needed to preach the Gospel, to love. Where are they? Where are the missionaries for whom the whole world clamors? Why are we always so far behind?

Perhaps because we have forgotten that, as Christ said, unless the grain of wheat falls into the ground and dies, it remains alone. But if it dies, it brings forth much fruit. We have not died to our selfishness. We refuse to love. We refuse to be channels of grace, of God's love. We make little use of the opportunities given to us to love.

There may be many saints living today, but there are always too few saints. To die to self, to love — this is a favorite theme of all spiritual writers, of all who speak or write about the apostolate in our own day. Seasoned missionaries put it this way: "The central problem of a missionary's challenge is to die to his own way of life so as to present the true face of Christ to people who belong to another way of life." These are strong words which go to the very heart of the matter and clearly define the essence of every apostolate, and of the Christian life itself.

For every Christian has been constituted an apostle by Baptism and by Confirmation. Every Christian has the right and the duty to help others reach salvation. Every Christian has been sent on a glorious mission. He lives in the world to speak the words of Another, to accomplish the plans of Another, to bring the love of Another incarnated in his own heart.

Fruits there will be, but measured by the increase of *caritas*, true supernatural love, if the Christian strives valiantly to die each day to self. If he loves with a truly oblative love, the love of the false self will most surely die the death. God makes this possible by placing in us the power to love. Of ourselves we can do nothing.

Christ died to self before dying on the cross. In the luminous words of St. Paul: "Though he was in the form of God...he emptied himself and took the form of a slave, being born in the likeness of men" (Phil. 2:6-7). "Your attitude must be that of Christ" (Phil. 2:5). Let this attitude be in us! Let us empty ourselves, and the power of God's love, working through us His representatives, will fill the world.

Every Christian is an apostle, a sharer in the priesthood of Christ, capable of becoming a powerfully productive member of His Body. Every Christian is needed in the gigantic struggle for the minds and hearts of men. The apostolate cannot be limited to only a few. All men are called to a life of love. All those who are confirmed have been given the power of *caritas* and the joyful responsibility of spreading

it throughout the whole world. We must have faith
for this task, a dynamic appreciation of what we are.
God has made us great. God has empowered our
weakness with His power. What are we doing with it?

Pusillanimity—a faintheartedness, timidity—this
may well be our greatest problem. We are afraid to
venture, afraid to live, afraid to die, afraid to love,
afraid to move. We are tepid. Like lukewarm tea unfit
to drink. Nauseating. Many people reject us. Many
cultures throw us up. Too few there are in the world
who desire to drink the Christian cup. We have
offered them ourselves, our thoughts, our way of
life, our culture. We have not died to all those things,
and so we have presented to them, not Christ, but
a poor substitute, a deformed Christ.

Too often we have gauged our apostolic efforts
by temporal and worldly success: prestige, status,
wealth. There have been some heroes of the Cross.
There have also been coattail-riders of imperialism
both at home and abroad.

Charles de Foucauld went to the desert and
atoned. He died to self, to his own culture, his
own way of life. He offered his love to God and
God's love to all who came by. So can each one of us
do. In the "desert" of one's home, office, or factory,
peacefully and joyfully, we can die to ourselves,
knowing that we are building up the Body of Christ,
and that we already share in the glory of His resurrection.

Christians of the world, arise! You have nothing
to lose but your fears.

God's
Concern is
Unity

"I do not pray for them alone.
I pray also for those who will believe in me through
 their word,
that all may be one
as you, Father, are in me and I in you;
I pray that they may be one in us,
that the world may believe that you sent me" (Jn.
17:20-21).

The Lord Jesus Christ, just before He suffered
and passed over to the Father, prayed with a loud cry,
springing up from the depths of His great heart and
soul. He asked that we should receive a large share
of His most God-like gift: unity, oneness, and the love
which makes us one. God is love. He is three Persons,
but the three are so united that there is only one God.
The very essence of God is love, oneness, unity,
togetherness.

He has created man according to His image. We
who are many — millions — are to become one body
in Christ, one Person, as it were, united by bonds
of forgiveness and love. That is the good news the
Church preaches: we have been reconciled to the
Father in Jesus Christ and reconciled to each other,

11

if only we will accept this fact by believing in the Lord Jesus and entering His kingdom.

On the other hand, nothing is more disastrous, nothing is more contrary to the whole movement of God's purpose than division, separation, opposition, hatred, alienation of one man from another.

The lines of battle are clearly drawn within our own hearts. Deep within me is a yearning for oneness, for communication with God and with other people, a great hunger for love. On the other hand there often rises in me anger, arrogance, the desire to be superior and "first," a limitless capacity for being annoyed with my brother, a fear of being forever alone. Will my allegiance be to love or to hatred, to union or to division? In this, essentially, do I find the struggle of every day.

I have asked myself, "What must I do to be an agent of union among men?" After much thought and prayer the answer came to me: "Pray for humility so that you will always see clearly and acknowledge easily the causes of disunity in your own heart, in your own life. See where you fail and ask God to correct that." Then I considered the Lord Jesus Christ and realized that He, who of all people brought union and peace most effectively, gave us the secret of doing likewise when He said: "There is no greater love than this: to lay down one's life for one's friends" (Jn. 15:13).

This is the price of unity, the price of peace among men, the price of total reconciliation. Each day I have the opportunity of laying down my life for my friends in many little ways — by prayer, service, and by the duty of the moment, but also by my reactions to my neighbor, for instance, when I am annoyed. Instead of expressing my hostility or retaliating, I can die at that moment simply by turning

the other cheek, listening to my neighbor, letting
the annoyance go. In so doing I will suffer a little;
indeed I will die a little.

And through such dying, God will give me
moments of peace—and they will be shared by my
friends.

"Father,
all those you gave me
I would have in my company
where I am,
to see this glory of mine
which is your gift to me,
because of the love you bore me before the world
    began" (Jn. 17:24).

How great our responsibility, how great our privilege, to give flesh to the power of God's love by letting it take hold of our own hearts. God's love will be
"unemployed" unless we bring it to earth. Let us
open our hearts wide to the power of His love, that it
may spread like a fire on our earth.

The Return of Prayer and Hidden Kindness

"If anyone says, 'My love is fixed on God,'
yet hates his brother,
he is a liar.
One who has no love for the brother he has seen
cannot love the God he has not seen.
The commandment we have from him is this:
whoever loves God must also love his brother" (1 Jn.
4:20-21).

As Catherine Doherty has often said, "The Christian is cruciform. With one hand he touches God, with the other he touches his neighbor." He witnesses before men to the existence of a transcendent God revealed to us by Jesus; for the God we worship is the Father of our Lord Jesus Christ, who has revealed Himself in His Son and sent us His Spirit to be our guide and comforter. The God we bow to is trinitarian, Father, Son, and Holy Spirit. The Christian also witnesses to Jesus, the servant of all, who said, "I have come to serve and not to be served."

During the years following the Vatican Council II, thousands of priests, religious, and young people were deeply moved by the Spirit to devote themselves to the works of mercy, social justice, peace among men. Thousands went to underdeveloped countries or to underdeveloped areas in their own countries to minister enthusiastically to the needs "of the poor." In the process, in many instances, the transcendent God was forgotten, prayer neglected, and devotions dropped.

Now we are bringing about a resurgence of prayer. The transcendent God – Father, Son and Holy Spirit – once again reveals Himself to thousands. Once again Catholic periodicals discuss prayer. Thousands of people are turning to the Bible for direction and sustenance. Meditation is enjoying a new popularity.

For years I have had a dream, that capitalists, socialists, economists, labor leaders—under God and with much prayer—would finally assemble and work out solutions to the problems of poverty and war. Will this ever happen? Will men ever meet together as brothers to take care of the needs of all, no longer merely favoring the privileged few? What a service these specialists might give their brothers and sisters who live on the edge of despair!

We may not be called to such service at a world level, but each of us has constant opportunities for prayer and for bringing a little happiness to somebody else. What the world needs is thousands of little people in thousands of little places doing thousands of little things for others.

Marie of the Incarnation writes: "For many years I worked as the servant of my brother's servants. I did secretly what they were supposed to do,

so that when they came to do it, they found it done."
And at the end of his life, St. Vincent de Paul was
asked what he would like to have done that he
hadn't done. He simply answered, "More."

Jesus gives us the secret of life, and the secret
is *love*. Fulfillment, happiness comes to the one
who loves God and neighbor, to the one who loses
himself in prayer and service of others. According
to one spiritual writer, the highest prayer consists
simply in being aware of God's existence, your
existence, and in offering yourself to Him. The
exercise can be summarized: "I am. You are. Here
I am." Try it sometime!

Let us pray that all men be moved to use the
power which Jesus brought to our world. Not the
power of wealth or of human wisdom, not the power
of weapons or show of force, but the power of love,
the love which loses its life for others.

Parents –
Reflecting
(Blocking?)
God's Love

Among good Christians
the word "love" produces a variety of reactions
and connotations: love of God, love of neighbor,
God is love. Many good people who have spent
their lives trying to know, love, and serve God
faithfully fear that they do not love Him. Others
equate love with gushing emotions, possessiveness,
a crippling sentimentality. Still others rejoice at the
thought that God is love, and that He has given
them at Baptism the power to love Him and to love
their neighbors.

I suggest that two principal causes explain
these reactions: one is psychological and the other
is theological. Let us consider the psychological
first.

To become a mature, stable, loving adult, a child
needs tender, strong, enlightened and unselfish love
of both his father and his mother. If this has not
been given even though the father and mother are
not at fault—you can expect trouble in later life.
Sooner or later, fears, anxieties, guilt feelings, feelings of inadequacy, depressions, resentments—all

17

these, latent since childhood, will come to the surface and create havoc.

The man or woman who is afraid of God may have missed out on strong, tender, enlightened, unselfish love from his father. If the father was hard to please, if it was "impossible to please him," then we may grow up feeling "unworthy" of approval, unable to be satisfied with any accomplishment in any field, including our life with God. In other words, it becomes well-nigh impossible to believe in God's love. The relationship develops on our part as one of fear, and the thought of death is likely to produce panic, so true is it that our emotions function in symbols.

To a child his father is god, strong, omnipotent, all-wise. He protects, nourishes, gives security. Life is livable only if he is on your side, if he is there to sustain you as you grow up and face your first painful encounters with reality. So small is the child, and so inadequate is the adolescent, and so big and terrifying is the world, that a strong man (the father) is needed to advise him, direct him, help him to gradually stand on his own two feet.

Without this man who believed in him, who approved of him, who was pleased at his efforts, an adult faces reality, the simple reality of everyday living, filled with apprehensions and gnawing anxieties. And since his father "has let him down," he is automatically fearful that God also is letting him down, that God does not care, that God also is hard to please and dissatisfied with his best efforts.

If fear of God can often be attributed to a deficiency in the father, the emotional rejection of love is frequently due to the mother, to the well-known evil called *momism.* The essence of momism is that the mother, because of her own insecurity, loves the child for her own sake, for herself. She latches on to him for her own emotional satisfaction. As he grows up, the child resents this bitterly. He moves away from her when she wants to embrace him, for he feels, unconsciously but deeply, that his mother loves herself in him and not *him*. And the word love becomes nauseating, repulsive, until the day he meets a true love, someone who really cares for him, or until he sees a psychiatrist (or, often, a priest) who helps him see and understand.

Such a man is predisposed to feeling that the love of God is also selfish, crippling, possessive (in the wrong sense) and he may never know the freedom of the children of God. Further, he is inclined to seek for a mother in his wife, to let her run the family, and to behave as a child. Skid row is full of "momma boys." Often it will be most difficult for him (or her) to have any devotion to our Lady, to believe in her tender, strong, unselfish love. Love to him means being eaten up emotionally by the one who should feed him.

There is absolutely no question here of blaming parents, of judging them harshly. Were they themselves mature, able to give love, or had they entered marriage already more or less crippled emotionally, it is not for us to say. And no man is to blame anybody for his own problems, since, in the loving providence of God, we've had the parents that we've had *only for a greater love*.

But fathers and mothers of this generation have little excuse for not utilizing the knowledge at hand to ensure for their children that emotional stability upon which grace may more easily build. If you love your children, it will be easier for them to believe in the love of God and of our Lady, and easier for them to love God and to love their neighbor.

We Sometimes Carry the Wrong Crosses

A man was walking down a road carrying a heavy burden on his back. His step was slow, his breathing labored, his body bent with the weight of his load. He stumbled, fell, tried to get up but the last ounce of energy had been drained from his body and the last drop of courage from his spirit. He sat there in the dust weeping bitter tears, bemoaning his lot and, like Job, cursing the day of his birth.

And then the gentle Lord appeared to him. "Why do you sit here, weeping and cursing, bemoaning your lot?" He asked softly. "Tell me your cares, share with me the sorrows of your heart."

And the man answered: "This pack I am made to carry all the days of my life; this heavy load of crosses is more than I can bear. Would that I could continue this journey manfully and without complaint, but Your holy will is hard. You demand far too much of human nature. I beg You, remove these

20

crosses with which You have laden my life." In fear
and trembling he bent low in the dust before the Lord
Almighty, awaiting punishment and rebuke for
speaking so boldly.

But the Lord went to him, lifted the pack from the
tired shoulders, and gave him His hand. "Rise," He
said, "let us examine these crosses you claim have
come from my will." The bag was opened, revealing
its assortment of black and gray crosses, and a small
one, light and shiny. "This one is from me," He said.
"All the others are of your own making. Throw them
out and you will understand that my yoke is easy and
my burden light."

The man did just that. He threw away all the
black crosses and all the gray crosses, threw the bag
away, and tied the one small, shiny cross around his
neck. He kissed the Lord's feet reverently and pro-
ceeded on his journey with a smile on his lips and a
song in his heart.

There is suffering in our lives, but perhaps much
of it is of our own making. The Lord has told us
that *His* yoke is easy and *His* burden light. Our
suffering is often due to not getting what we want.
We become frustrated, resentful, hostile to our
environment and to the people in it, and we become
depressed. These negative reactions, these painful
feelings result from our craving for things we should
not have or cannot have. The evil consists mainly in
having desires which nothing or no one can fulfill
or should fulfill. We attempt to satisfy our hunger
for happiness with things which are unable to nourish us.

Therefore, much pain can be avoided if we throw
away all our desires except one — the desire to do the
will of the Beloved, of God. This mental attitude,
based upon faith and trust in His goodness and power,

will gradually lead us to Him without having to carry the heavy baggage of misguided desires—our black and gray crosses—leaving us with only the small, shiny cross willed for us by God. Christ tells us to "seek first his kingship over you, his way of holiness" (Mt. 6:33), and He assures us "that all these things will be given" to us (Mt. 6:33). He assures us that this is the way—singleness of purpose—which will lead us to a great union of love with Him.

Our joy as Christians is often weak. Yet the Christian has every reason to rejoice. All through the Gospels—which is the Good News, not the bad news—the Lord explains over and over to His disciples that they are to find their joy and their happiness in the midst of poverty, of tears, of sorrows, and of persecutions.

Blessed are the poor; God's reign is theirs. Blessed are those who hunger; they shall be filled. Blessed are those weeping; they shall laugh. Blessed will they be whom men hate, whom they ostracize and insult, and whose name they proscribe as evil because of the Son of Man. Their reward shall be great in heaven.

The Christian is told that he must not consider poverty, sorrow, hunger and persecution as obstacles to his joy, but rather that if they come into his life, he should find therein his happiness. In fact he can possess true joy even while feeling pain and depression. If he tries feverishly, frantically, unpeacefully to solve these problems or to escape from all pain, he will be plagued by frustration. Life for such a one becomes grim and the law of God which is all love becomes harsh and impossible to bear. A sad Christian has not sufficiently grasped the essentials of his faith.

We have many other reasons for rejoicing amid the difficulties and tribulations which are the common lot of fallen human nature. Christ has taken upon Himself the major portion of our atonement. He carried mankind's cross and left us only a little splinter as our share. He triumphed over death so that we could face death with hope of eternal life. He resurrected from the dead so that we too could resurrect one day in glory. And for our journey on earth He clothed our impoverished humanity with the warm and shining robe of His grace. To fight the enemy, He has filled us with strength. To satisfy our hunger, He gives us Himself as food as often as we want Him. To make each day a glorious one, His grace is offered profusely to all men of good will whereby the humblest action is transformed into a thing of beauty. His love surrounds us, enfolds us, warms us every step of the way.

Is a joyless Christian really a Christian? He lives not by faith but by natural values. He should assess his desires, his faith, and take the words of Christ to heart: "Seek first his kingship over you, his way of holiness, and all things will be given you besides" (Mt. 6:33).

Love alone, illumined by faith and strengthened by hope, can make us seek the one thing necessary: union with the Beloved. If we strive each day to live in love, patiently, kindly, seeking not our own will but only the will of the Beloved, then we shall get rid of our multitudinous desires, our frustrations, and all the useless crosses we carry around on our backs. Love is a power. It has the power to reject, to eliminate our wayward desires in the measure in which we let it free to focus upon one desire: union with the Beloved according to His will.

Why Be Sad When Loved by God?

Let us talk about joy some more, for there is so much joy in our lives and yet so many of us seem to be unaware of that joy. Joy is the fruit of love. Joy fills a heart when it possesses the object of its love, when its desires have been fulfilled. Why do so many Christians seem joyless? Perhaps because they do not realize that they possess and are possessed by God.

Joy is the result of peace, when all things are in order, when we realize our misery, our utter poverty, and have learned to depend for all things on God's infinite mercy.

God is He-who-gives-Himself-always. He gives Himself to me right now—everything that He is. He comes to satisfy all my needs, to fulfill all my desires. He comes humbly, entering into the chambers of my soul only as far as I will let Him. He wants me to become like Him, to be self-giving, so that I may enjoy His presence. He desires to be united with me as intimately as steel is united with fire. He comes to bring me joy.

The Christian overflows with reasons for rejoicing. The Old Testament revealed God as the Lover of mankind. The Gospel reveals the depths of that love. The Church Christ founded makes us one with Him at Baptism, provides us through her sacraments with powerful means for deeper union with our Beloved and with one another, and prepares us for that most joyful, final encounter after death. All around us His creation shines forth with beauty and shouts of His tenderness, from the awesome reaches of space to the breath-taking glory of a drop of water.

There is joy when we know that He whom we love loves us, and that our Lover does not make us wait for union. Forever He stands at our door, waiting for us to open to Him. At every moment we can meet with Him. A high point of meeting is at the Eucharist.

At the Eucharist Christ takes us to Himself and brings us with Him into the secret heart of God. Tenderly He places us with Himself in the bosom of the Father. At the Eucharist we rise from earth to live in the very Source of our origin. We who came from the hand of Love now return to our beginnings, the heart of the Father.

At the Eucharist Christ feeds our hunger with Himself. In truth, we do receive Him who is our Beloved and the Lover of our souls. We receive Him in His immense fullness, body, blood, soul, and divinity. This is the greatest moment of union, the greatest union on earth. It is, therefore, the greatest moment of Joy; we possess and are possessed. The All is with us and we are in the All, one with Him and with each other in Him. This is our greatest joy on earth. We thirst for love and Love has come to us.

Our emptiness screams to be filled, and Infinite Love does come to fill us to overflowing.

How can a Christian be sad if he has faith, if he has humility, if he lives in the truth? Our misery attracts Infinite Love as an empty canyon attracts the wayward wind. This is joy, to realize that Infinite Love swoops down to fill all our chambers if only we open them wide to Him. Here is Christian joy!

Each day Christ waits at the place of meeting. Each day we may possess perfect joy. For each day we can be possessed and possess. How grateful we should be to the Church, our Mother, the Fair Bride of Christ, for all the love and concern with which she has surrounded the Eucharist down through the ages!

The Eucharist will become the great moment of joy in our lives in the measure in which we appreciate our need, our neighbor, and the infinite love of God. It will take us "out of ourselves." Let us learn how to rejoice at the Eucharist.

Joy fills us when we are united with our Beloved, with our Lover. We can be united with Him at all times, right now in fact. But our communion is especially intense at the Eucharist when we meet Him together with our brothers and sisters. There He lifts us all to the bosom of the Father who is our origin, our life, our destiny. Such is the power of love, the power of the God who is love.

Love: He-Who-Gives-Himself

A Christian is one who loves. That is his distinctive mark or characteristic. He is not merely one who fasts, or who goes to church, or who reads spiritual books, but one who loves. "Walk in love," says St. Paul. "By this will all men know that you are my disciples, if you have love for one another." The Lord taught this lesson many times in many different words and deeds all through His life. Love God, love your neighbor. These few words summarize the whole of the Christian life.

To love is to give all that one possesses and all that one is. God, who is love, gives all that He possesses and all that He is, first in creation and more fully in the Person of the Son. We are called to imitate Christ, and we do so by self-giving, by loving.

Love is the life of the Most Holy Trinity. The Father gives Himself perfectly to His Son, the Son to His Father, and this mutual gift eternally flowers into the Holy Spirit. God is He-who-is-always-self-giving. This was the essence of Christ's revelation. He came to tell us that God loves us. He spoke in deeds much more than in words.

Every action of the Boy, the Carpenter, the Preacher, the Healer, spelled out for all to see that God gives not only His power, His talents, His knowledge, but always Himself, and all of Himself. On the cross, for three excruciating hours, He proclaimed the message in all its fullness. Who is God? Look. Read the clear answer in each precious drop of His blood. In ringing tones they chant as they flow: "God is He-who-gives-Himself-always!"

This was the moment of His great glory. On the previous night He had anticipated it by exclaiming:

"Father, the hour has come!
Give glory to your Son
that your Son may give glory to you..." (Jn. 17:1).

He rose triumphant on Easter morning. He appeared to His apostles in His transfigured body, joyfully bearing eloquent wounds, five great proofs of God's love. Gazing in awe upon these five most precious jewels, the apostles knew that He who had suffered and died on Friday was indeed God. And they learned that God is He-who-is-always-giving-Himself, totally, and without reservation.

They were stunned. They had expected Christ to manifest His power in other ways: by calling on His angels, by pulverizing His enemies, by proclaiming Himself King, by making them rich, powerful, important. But now all that was terribly changed. What did *His kind* of self-giving mean for them? That they would have to give of themselves even unto death? That they would have to become servants instead of masters? That they should become vulnerable to offenses by offering the other cheek and by loving their enemies?

I think they were certainly stunned, being human, just as we are stunned when He-who-gives-

Himself-always looks at us, shows us His wounds, and asks: "Do you want to become divine?" We can't take it, and Peter couldn't take it either. Of course he rejoiced that the Lord had conquered death. But now he, Peter, had to conquer the world, he as the rock. He had begun to suspect the price of that conquest. He couldn't face it. We know that he went back fishing!

What thoughts must have harassed him during those strange days which preceded the transforming action of the Spirit of Love. Mechanically, Peter repeated the gestures of the past: fishing, eating, sleeping, pretending nothing had really changed. Perhaps he saw again all the unpleasant events of the last few days and years — the persecutions, the animosities of the ruling classes, the misunderstandings, the constant opposition, the humiliations, the sufferings. And now, all these things *without* Christ to carry the load, to sustain, to encourage, to lead.

Good-bye plans of a glorious kingdom on earth! Good-bye prestige, honor, and position! A life like Christ's, and perhaps a death like His! Peter kept on fishing — but only for a while. Then he followed in Christ's footsteps. He died joyfully embracing his own special cross.

God is He-who-always-gives-Himself. God invites us to imitate Him. He invites us to a union of total love. He invites us to love, to give of ourselves. He invites us, in short, to suffer, to die to self, to put to death our self-love by loving. Like the apostles, we too are stunned, dazed, when we begin to "get the picture." We want to run away, to distract ourselves, to forget. We fear with a great fear, we tremble, we try to fight it off whenever an "impossible" love is asked of us, whenever we feel tested beyond human endurance, whenever the cross seems to be intolerable.

We need to pray then, to pray as never before, even if all we can offer is the prayer of our tears, the prayer of our fears, the prayer of our cowardice. Perhaps "our hour has not yet come," as a modern writer has put it. We should pray, he continues, not only to be resigned to God's will, but to embrace joyfully this new challenge to our love, this bright and shining opportunity for a greater self-giving.

We become God-like in the measure in which we give ourselves, in the measure in which we love, in the measure in which we are always giving ourselves. This is the power of love. It makes us God-like. It makes us like Him-who-is-always-giving-Himself.

Is Christ Relevant?

Is Christ relevant? Is the Church relevant? Is the priest relevant? Is the Catholic relevant? Is God Himself relevant? Many assert that God, Christ, religion, the Church, have nothing to do with men and women of the twentieth century, people "come of age." It is a common belief that man has no need of God, that through the various sciences he can take care of all his problems. He has technology to feed him and psychology to bring him peace of mind. He is able to experience deep satisfaction by communicating with other people. Men can now fulfill themselves!

Yet, each one of you reading this book knows for himself his need for Someone beyond people and things, a longing for the Infinite, a yearning for a union which nothing human can accomplish. Christ is as relevant as ever, perhaps more so than ever. Men today are keenly aware of their fears, their emptiness, their abysmal loneliness. Their wounds cry out for healing beyond human healing, and their hunger only deepens as they experience human love. They know in their hearts that they need Christ, that they need a Father all powerful and loving, and that they need a Spirit to guide them to this Father.

Christ alone is the answer to our basic fears. Fears of death, dissolution, of going to pieces. Christ alone is the answer to our emptiness and loneliness. Christ alone gives meaning to suffering and frustration. Indeed, "You have made us for Yourself, O Lord, and our hearts are restless until they rest in You." These words of St. Augustine are as true today as on the day they were first uttered, for they resound deeply in our own hearts.

Yes, God and His Christ are as relevant as ever, but how shall we meet them? They seem sometimes to be absent from our world. We meet them by listening to the Scriptures with eager hearts, praying to the Holy Spirit to make the words contained therein vital, healing, and strengthening for us. "God's word is living and effective, sharper than any two-edged sword. It penetrates and divides soul and spirit, joints and marrow; it judges the reflections and thoughts of the heart. Nothing is concealed from him; all lies bare and exposed to the eyes of him to whom we must render an account" (Heb. 4:12-13).

We meet Christ at that memorial He told us to celebrate in His name: the Eucharist. "The liturgy in its turn moves the faithful, filled with 'the paschal sacraments,' to be 'one in holiness'; it prays that 'they may hold fast in their lives to what they have grasped by their faith'; the renewal in the eucharist of the covenant between the Lord and man draws the faithful into the compelling love of Christ and sets them on fire. From the liturgy, therefore, and especially from the eucharist, as from a font, grace is poured forth upon us; and the sanctification of men in Christ and the glorification of God, to which all other activities of the Church are directed as toward their end, is achieved in the most efficacious possible way" (Constitution on the Sacred Liturgy, n. 10).

Thirdly, Christ is met in the service of others. Service, as a sign of love, contains within itself perfection. The Christians who serve their neighbors are free at that moment from selfishness. Christ has made them free. He is then united with them, and they meet Christ in others. *Whatever you do to the least of my brothers* is not mere poetry. It is reality to the one who has faith. We meet Christ in others.

May the power of Christ's love and life in Christians go forth today throughout the whole world, bringing His healing peace and joy — His relevance! — to millions.

World's
Best Kept
Secret

Our society is in ferment. Men and nations are restless, for in no field of human endeavor is there to be found that assurance in the truth, that stability which makes for peace and order in a town, a nation, or the world.

Man has definite needs: food, clothing, shelter, education, health, recreation, peace. These needs are poorly satisfied today. In education, economic and international affairs, family life, the truth has often been abandoned to opinions, experiments, accomodations motivated most frequently by selfishness of one type or another. The predominant philosophy is basically the same in both East and West: materialism.

The problem is a religious one. We Christians have forgotten to tell the truth and to live it. We have simply forgotten. Perhaps we have heard it so little that we have never really grasped it. The truth is that God is love, that He cares for us, that nothing happens but for a greater love, that the essence of religion is to love. These truths must be lived to make life on earth endurable and joyful.

34

If parents loved their children properly, there would be far less need for psychiatrists, doctors, and hospitals. Juvenile delinquency would diminish considerably, as also the need for correctional institutions, law courts, and jails. If employer and employee made a serious attempt to love one another (to consider the other fellow's point of view), and if nations loved one another, gradually solid solutions would be found to our vexing economic problems.

Without love it is impossible to see reality as it is. Without love the most brilliant plans of the most brilliant minds fall short of the truth. To organize the world without love is to organize it without God who is truth; and the truth about Him is that He is love. This is the truth which many Christians have forgotten.

Too rarely do we remember that God is love, that He cares, that obedience, chastity, humility, mortification, are means to a greater love affair with the Crucified. Too rarely do we remember that by loving other men we can assuage His pain in them and find the power to love for another day. Ask yourself: "How often have I examined my conscience on love? How often have I told my children that God loves them? Do I believe that God loves *me?* Do I believe that all He wants from me is my love, that He thirsts for my love?"

Repeatedly, through the years, I have met with graduates from Catholic colleges and high schools. They were concerned about many things, such as sex, politics, economics, morality. There were many questions and discussions on these important subjects. There were few discussions, however, on the love of God. So often their reaction to the statement, "God loves you," was one of uneasiness or disbelief. Yet for many years they had been exposed to religion. They knew many things and yet they knew very little. Some were scholars but they were not wise. They knew every tree in the forest but they had missed the woods. They were great men, but had not become as little children.

Simplicity is the highest wisdom. Simplicity, the little daughter of love, armed with the sword of truth, must cut through the jungle of complexities born of our intellectual pride and must lead us to the pearl of great price.

Simplicity is no more a simpleton than love is sentimental. Her characteristic is that she sees with clear eyes. Being without fear she is able to look at reality. Being without selfishness, her assessment of problems is objective. Being full of love, she uses all of man's faculties to analyze the ailment, find the cure, and work at it. Witness the truly great names of our day: St. Therese, Charles de Foucauld, St. Pius X. All of them were clothed in true simplicity.

No one is to be blamed specifically by us for the "evils in the world." Not even you and I. Our poor sins have been confessed and lavishly forgiven by the God who is love. What is needed is a shift of emphasis to *love*. Let love be lived by employer and employee and they will find equitable solutions. Let love be lived and taught by parents, teachers, and priests, and the Spirit will renew the face of the land. But the price is high, for love leads inevitably to the cross where hangs Love Itself.

Christ's words are so clear:

" 'You shall love the Lord your God....

You shall love your neighbor as yourself.'

On these two commandments the whole law is based, and the prophets as well" (Mt. 22:37-40). All truths are contained in love and emanate from love — for God is love.

Truth –
Painful But
Healing

Peace and love grow in a soul or an environment where humility is firmly rooted in faith. For humility is the virtue of truth, the virtue which reveals to us the truth about ourselves. It shows us our weaknesses, our limitations, our nothingness, our need for total dependence on God, our need for His grace and His sustaining strength.

A humble man rejoices at the sight of his weaknesses and begins to appreciate the words of Christ: *Without me you can do nothing.* He begins to rely on that strength, confident that it will never fail. He becomes strong with a strength that is not his own. He becomes fearless and dauntless in the face of overwhelming difficulties, solidly anchored in the power of God's love.

Humility makes us face the truth. A false peace covers the world, penetrates into families, parishes, and convents. Many people equate peace with an absence of turmoil. For them, it is a negative thing. It avoids all unpleasantness, all facing of the truth. It wants to leave well enough alone. It lets sleeping

37

dogs lie. It is satisfied with apparent order, that superficial coating which so often hides much disorder.

True peace may exist in apparent turmoil...when the contending parties are sincerely seeking to know the will of God and are committed in their hearts to that holy will. For peace is the product of order, real order, and humility is the enemy of disorder.

The Lord says that He brings not peace, but the sword. He speaks of the sword of truth which cuts through the illusions, delusions, and the infinite rationalizations which the self throws up as so many impregnable walls for its own protection. And while we are busy protecting ourselves, putting up our barriers, striving for pleasant situations, disorder grows and true peace vanishes.

Knowledge of self and knowledge of God have always been held in high esteem by spiritual writers. They are classical means to union with God. The first is the product of humility and achieved by examination of conscience; the second is due to faith and achieved by fidelity to mental prayer. Daily experience well assessed shows us our weakness, our inadequacies, our contingency. Daily mental prayer reveals to us that God is love, that He is our Father, that He is merciful, that our misery attracts His mercy, providing we acknowledge that misery. God resists the proud, the self-sufficient, for pride twists the truth, shapes it to our own advantage. It is the enemy of God, for God is truth.

Let us not fear the truth, painful as it often is to face. It leads to peace, joy, and love. It will reveal many things. It will reveal our need for personal redemption, the deep realization that our personal sinfulness can only be healed by Christ. It will reveal the joy of being redeemed, that Christ has died for me so that I might live and be a child of God.

The truth will reveal our need of other people. It will give us a clear appreciation of all the things we daily receive from others — food, clothing, shelter, knowledge, art, friendship, spiritual help. It will make us see that we cannot live without the constant support of the rest of the human race.

The truth will expose our rationalizations. How often do we do the right thing for the right reason, or find good reasons for doing the wrong thing! Afraid to look at our weakness, to admit our insecurity to ourselves or to anybody else, we keep busy, we dare not stop our work or our play. We have explanations all ready, all kinds of explanations for our behavior — some wrong, some closer to the truth, some in accordance with reality. That is why the psalmist invites us to pray to be delivered from our *secret sins*, our secret selfishness, that grasping part of self of which we may be unaware.

To love is to give oneself — not only one's talents, one's work, one's service, but *oneself* — without seeking a return. That is a sublime love and it can develop only in a person who is somewhat aware of the self's multiple deceptions.

True humility is a gift from God, a painful grace, because the sight of our misery hurts. We thought ourselves to be loving, pleasant, dedicated people, and, lo and behold, God, through people and pressures, lets us see our resentments, the coldness of our hearts, the smallness of our loves.

This is a grace, a time of growth, a grand opportunity. Desolate, shaken, at times terrified, let us pray for faith and courage, let us look at God, at Christ. Let us turn to our Lady in our abysmal need. She will lead us through the valley of humility to the fair country of peace, of joy and of love. At first the valley seems cold, stark, harsh, but gradually it turns into a rich and pleasant garden.

To love without seeking a return for one's love, to give ourselves without thought of self, that is true *caritas* whose power overcomes evil and spreads God's kingdom upon the earth. That is redemptive love, man's most valuable contribution to God's glory and the salvation of souls, the love which moves weak human beings to accomplish the impossible, the love which makes extraordinary the most ordinary actions.

At the sight of her nothingness made great by the love of God, our Lady broke into song. We too can sing her Magnificat when we become conscious of our nothingness and conscious of the wonders which God operates in us.

Spirit's A-movin' — Are We?

We are fortunate to be living at this time in history when the Holy Spirit, the Spirit of truth and of love, is moving powerfully through the land. This powerful, passionate, impatient Spirit of love blows mightily wherever He wills. A new Pentecost is upon us, and our days are filled with a promise, a hope, a burgeoning of love. We witness Him moving through thousands, millions of hearts — restless, seeking hearts, hearts of men of good will throughout the world who yearn for social justice, for peace, for love, for God.

Let us respond fearlessly and passionately to His love. He comes to transform, to revitalize, to renew the face of our earth. He invites us not to be afraid of having our lives "overhauled" by His breath. Love is at the helm. Love leads the way. Love is the maker, the way, and the end of this

41

movement. We need to open our hearts to love, to God. We are asked to follow His lead. We need to break our stony hearts which the Spirit will replace with hearts of flesh.

Truly, the Spirit is on the move. Are we moving with Him? And if we answer "Yes," the next question is, "How much?" God has many acquaintances, less friends, still less lovers, and only a handful of passionate lovers. To which class do we belong?

The Holy Spirit's work of renewal can only be accomplished by renewed persons. Through them He will renew the face of the earth. Am I in this process of renewal, am I "with it," am I fully in the swift-flowing current of grace? Why am I so slow to respond to this tremendous Lover? I mean, fully respond, with all that I am and all that I have. Why do I make excuses? Why do I rationalize away the Spirit's insistent presence in my life? Why do I refuse to let the fire consume me?

The Spirit blows mightily. He blows at the door of my heart. My door, it is true, is unlocked; it is open perhaps a crack. But I hesitate to throw it wide open. Every chilly gust tends to shut it again. How long can I refuse to admit this persistent Lover and keep asking, "Is it really You?"

How many passionate lovers will it take to renew the face of the earth? And where are these lovers, these pure channels and transmitters of His love? Am I, are you, such a one for whom both God and man hunger? By what miracle will the door of my heart finally be kicked in to welcome God and man?

The homeless Spirit roams the land, seeking someone to love, someone to set on fire with love, seeking for a Bride, someone to renew and transform. Will I, will you, welcome Him? And when? Why wait any longer? Why make Him wait any longer who comes to fulfill every desire?

The homeless Spirit is all love. He brings nothing but love. He knows nothing but love. Love is His only name. Why wait? His longing to share His love with us, to pour it into us, surpasses by far any and all of the longings of the whole human race. "I am thirsty," Christ moaned on the cross (Jn. 19:28). Who shall give God satisfaction? Who will receive the gifts of the great Giver?

Disturbing
Young
Prophets

The "new breed" of young people desire community, deep personal relationships, and a living witness to Christ from those of us who claim to believe in Him. This new breed loves to talk, to discuss a multitude of subjects, to ask questions. And these young people will not be influenced by mere words, argumentation, and fine phrases. They demand much more of a believer. They want to see the truths he teaches take flesh in his own life. They want to touch his faith as it shapes, directs, and transforms his daily actions. They call for a kind of Gospel witness that is cried out not so much by one's mouth as by his life.

For those of us who are mediocre, complacent, unwilling to change, encrusted in a "safe and decent" type of Christianity, these young people constitute a threat. They annoy us. They disturb us. "Why do they question everything? Why aren't they like everybody else? Why aren't they satisfied with what we tell them? Why do they want to probe into my personal life and find out who I am?"

Annoying and disturbing as they may be at times, I believe that they are a gift from the Holy Spirit. They force us to think, to assess and reassess our values, to look at our lives with the penetrating and often cruel eyes of youth. Unknowingly they cry out the same words as St. John in his first letter: "Love not merely in theory or in words, love in sincerity and in practice." For this we can be grateful, even while appreciating that life will no longer be easy for the Christian.

We must be the salt of the earth, as Christ wants us to be, or else this generation will reject us and our message. We must let our light shine before men, or else they will lose their way in the enveloping gloom. We must love with the heart of Christ or else many will give themselves up to despair.

Christ the Lord brought the good news. He told us that we had a Father, that we were made for love, for union with Him and with one another. He became flesh, one of us, our brother, the first-born of a new race of men. He established His kingdom on our earth, a kingdom of peace, justice, love, truth, and mercy. A Christian strives to achieve these qualities in his own life. He strives to achieve them for all mankind—and all this, in spite of his personal selfishness, his poverty, his weakness, his struggle with sin. He is confident because he lives in the power of the risen Lord, because he trusts in God, because he strives daily to accomplish God's will at this moment of history.

The Holy Spirit is challenging us through the demands of our younger generation to practice what we preach, to show our faith in our deeds, to live what we claim to believe. The Holy Spirit hungers for the full incarnation, the continued and growing presence of the Word among men. He wants to penetrate the whole of reality, especially the reality of our own hearts. He yearns to spread the Gospel of peace and love through hearts that have become peace and love.

The twentieth century presents no easy challenge to the Christian, if indeed any century ever does. Christianity was never easy. Was it easy for the Lord? We know what happened to Him. He conquered, but at what a price! Who wants to pay that kind of a price?! Who wants to preach the Gospel with his life?! Who wants to bring peace and love to others?! Only a fool. But without such fools we die, and darkness conquers all. More than food and drink, men need the power of each other's love. May you be such a fool. May I be such a fool. May the Lord's love take flesh in our hearts.

Who Isn't
Poor?

It doesn't take much perception for a man to realize that he is full of imperfections. Daily his weakness manifests itself in thought, word, and deed. He smokes too much. He drinks too much. He runs away from unpleasant encounters. He works, but not too energetically. He is inclined to take too good care of himself. He is often sensitive, touchy, moody.

Pride, and all the other sins living within his heart, periodically break through the control of his will. This man is a Christian. He struggles. Good and evil battle within his breast. He is aware of the struggle. He knows his need for mercy and understanding, for forgiveness. He expects it from God and from neighbor.

Why then is he so intolerant of the weaknesses, the faults, the mistakes of others who share the same human condition and who also struggle with themselves? Surprising, isn't it? We need mercy and show so little mercy. We need forgiveness but demand payment for all offenses against us. We need to be understood, and have so little understanding for others!

47

Christ warned us about that, about this aspect of our blindness. St. Matthew records the parable of the unmerciful servant. A king wishes to settle accounts with his servants. One of them who owes him a huge sum of money pleads for mercy. The king graciously forgives him all and wipes the debt from the books. The forgiven man leaves the king's presence and meets a fellow servant who owes him a trifling sum. He demands payment on the spot, and has the poor man who is unable to pay thrown into prison! How often have we re-enacted this story in our own lives! Minutes, perhaps, after receiving absolution for our own sins, or after having been forgiven by another, we refuse to forgive!

Consider, in this connection, our attitude toward the poor — those favorite children of God who often lack food, clothes, and shelter. They live in the "tobacco rows" of America, trying to raise large families on small pensions, family allowances, or unemployment insurance. What are our attitudes toward them?

Those who have goods and who enjoy a certain material security have a tendency to condemn these people and to ignore their needs. The tendency is to consider them shiftless, lazy, and undependable. It is even remarked that "such people should not be allowed to have children to drain the economy."

People who are privileged to "help" the poor will tell you that they are far more helped by these very poor than they themselves give help. Christ has identified Himself with the unfortunate ones of the world. He said so. His powerful words are in the Gospel for all to read: "Come. You have my Father's blessing!... For I was hungry and you gave me food,... naked and you clothed me.... As often as you did it for one of my least brothers, you did it for me" (Mt.

25:34-40). The poor possess Christ's own power to bless and heal us. Truly they give us more than we give them.

"The poor are lazy," some say. So are rich people, and the reasonably comfortable—and all men. Ask people who work with the poor how often these men are desperately looking for work.

"The poor are ungrateful." So are the rich, and the reasonably comfortable—and all men. St. Vincent de Paul used to say to his Little Sisters of the Poor: "Do not give only a loaf of bread, but give it with a smile. And don't expect gratitude. It's hard enough being poor without having to be grateful about it!" But, to tell the truth, the poor are immensely grateful for food, clothing, furniture, and especially for friendship. And who will say that the well-to-do are more grateful for these things when they need them?

"Sometimes the poor take advantage of you." So do the rich, and the reasonably comfortable—and all men. These accusations toward the poor are simply variations on the theme of the unmerciful servant, and the tendency in us all to demand of others what we so grudgingly dole out to others.

Lord, merciful Lord of all, may the strength of Your love melt all hearts. Let us acknowledge that we are all poor, and completely dependent on You for all things. May we be merciful to everyone who is in need, and so enjoy Your mercy in heaven for eternity.

I'll Start Loving Next Year

Every year brings new challenges and new opportunities. Years may change but God remains ever the same — ever loving, ever giving, ever living. Every day He showers us with His gifts. I firmly believe that His gifts are not for tomorrow but for today. People say, "Some day I hope to be a saint. Some day I hope to be less selfish, more loving. Some day I'll look at the crucifix and realize what it means." How sad! Why wait for the good things of God? Why make *God* wait? Why reject His love today with the excuse that we will accept it tomorrow?

How much He desires to fill our hearts with His love! The waves of such love gently lap at the shores of our lives. His mighty heart beats close to our own. By our refusal to love now, we force the Spirit to contain His fire, while we go energetically about, seeking to make a life for ourselves, a life satisfied with drops of love when we could have oceans. O foolish men who search where they will not find, while the Best lies before them for the taking!

"Lord, make me wise. Give me some sense. I will set my heart on You. I will put my trust in You. I will open my hands and my heart at long last and allow You to fill them. I'm tired of being my own little god. I'm disgusted with my own little gifts to myself. I'm sorry I've made You wait so terribly long."

In the Bible we read the story of Israel. God made a covenant with these people. He asked for their loyalty, their trust. He promised unfailing protection and tender care. Frequently they refused His help, His gifts.

We read and we are shocked at their callous behavior. Have we a right to be shocked, to be appalled, to feel superior? Have we a right to be shocked since our behavior is so little different from theirs? And Christ has come to us; we have crucifixes in our homes and rooms; we have the Church and the Eucharist!

How many Christians alive today believe in God, the true God, the God of the living, of Abraham and Isaac and Jacob? The God of love and not only the God of wrath? The God who gives and not only the God who makes demands? The God who revealed Himself in Jesus Christ? How many trust Him in their daily lives? How many turn to Him with open hearts? How many follow His lead today? How many have the heart of a child? How many little ones are there in the world, those tremendous people who live in the power of His love?

But more to the point: Do *I* believe in God? I mean, in practice, in the concrete realities of the day, at work, at play, in my contacts with others. Right now am I aware of His care, of my total dependence upon His love? Now is the acceptable time, the time to receive gifts, the time of forgiveness. With God, *now* is always the right time.

"Lord, stir up my faith, sift the ashes, blow a mighty fire from its cooling embers! For You are God and I am a creature. You are He-who-is and I am he-who-is-not. You are power and I am weakness. You are wise and I am senseless. You are mercy and I am misery. Lord, stir up my faith."

In spite of appearances, God has not left our world. Millions have rejected Him but He has not rejected them. Communism denies the spiritual. Atheistic existentialism teaches men their nothingness, the absurdity of life. The accumulation of wealth leads to boredom. Anxiety, emptiness, frustration characterize our century. And fear, unnamable fear, surrounds us and saps our courage. But God has not abandoned us. It may well be that a purification of cosmic proportions is taking place in the hearts of men. As man becomes aware of his nothingness, he meets God. As man experiences his misery, he makes himself ready to experience mercy. As man becomes humble through confusion and distress, he comes closer to the truth — and God is truth.

Yes, challenging times we live in. The men of our generation are in pain. Their pain is of the spirit. They need us. They need our faith, our trust in God's care, our response to His love. In the abyss of nothingness where so many have been plunged, two hands are extended, the devil's and the Christian's. The first leads to final despair and destruction; the second to light, to peace, to joy — but it must be offered!

And God is there too, even in the abyss. We have nothing to fear. The power of His love will sustain us. This year, today, right now, let us believe in the power of God's love. His love, manifesting itself in human hearts, is powerful enough to save this generation so close to despair, but also so close to salvation.

The Spirit
Inspires
Trust

Jesus Christ is the center of human history. All creation tends toward Him. All things were made for Him. In Him, in Him alone, do we find our fulfillment, our completion, our joy. Through Him we have been reunited to our Father. The Holy Spirit sanctifies each person and the whole body of the faithful. He prepares us, transforms us each day for heaven, for eternal love, for an eternity of love.

Can we become like our Father who is love? Can we become loving persons? Yes, for He wants it. But not by ourselves. How then? By humble recourse to the Holy Spirit. He is the Sanctifier, the One who establishes loving relationships with the Father and with all our brothers.

Will He do this without our consent? No, for we are free beings. We are faced with a choice. God offers His love. We may accept or reject it. We may accept or reject His healing, consoling, strengthening activity. We may prefer to heal, console and strengthen ourselves. We may try to carry ourselves on our own shoulders, forgetting that we are creatures. We may act as if there were no God, as if we were gods.

What is the most that the Holy Spirit expects of a creature? He expects us *to pray to desire to trust in Him,* to pray to desire to do the will of the Father, to ask for His help and mercy at all times.

God wants to save us, to bring us to Himself, to create love among men. We have a loving Father, a loving Savior, a loving Sanctifier. Yet so often we try to do it all ourselves. So often we live as if we had no need of God, little realizing that every breath we take is a gift from Him, let alone our little acts of virtue.

We are constantly tempted to trust in ourselves rather than in Him, forgetting that the very reason and essence of God's revelation to us is that He is trustworthy, that He cares, that He alone is holy and the maker of saints.

How hard trust comes to us! How much easier it is to tackle our own problems by ourselves, to come to our own solutions, going from mess to mess, never solving anything. We play God in our lives. Thank God if we fail, for in our misery we will experience His mercy.

Trust—or faith, in the broad biblical sense—comes hard to proud human nature. Our basic choice consists in this: to live dependently upon God or independently; to acknowledge our essential poverty or to consider ourselves self-sufficient; to recognize our need or deny it; to live in the truth or in error. Will men be like gods, their own creators, their own redeemers, their own sanctifiers, or will they abandon themselves to Him-who-is and who is love? Will they seek His mercy and accept it? Will they trust in Him?

How difficult, how frightening, how humbling this basic truth of revelation! But mostly, how foolish we are to want so desperately to run our own show. Let us pray to the Holy Spirit, asking Him to reveal the Father to us, to reveal His love, His power, His concern, so as to live daily, in all our activities, within the power, the relaxing power of that love.

We Can
Heal Each
Other

Your home is love, and without love you gasp and die like a fish out of water. Your home is mercy, forgiveness, compassion. Without a friend to bind your wounds, you will never forgive yourself; without the healing mercy of God you will never have this strength to forgive either yourself or others. We can heal each other.

Parents can heal their children to some extent and open their hearts to the healing power of Christ who gives to each one of us the power of healing others.

We exist to be loved and to love. We know it, if we have stopped long enough to question our depths, to ask our own heart. We sense it, at least we sense something undefined, something unanswered, something missing. There is a dull ache, a passionate yearning, a dead hope wandering aimlessly around inside of us. I suspect that some of our frustration in communicating with each other is due to our need for love, our inability to trust another's love, a feeling that the other does not love me or does not appreciate my love.

A woman came to me with many theological questions. She spoke to me and to several other priests. She received what we thought were some adequate answers to her questions. But none of them satisfied her. The real question behind all the others was, "Do you respect me? Am I lovable?" Similarly a man discussed loudly all problems with assurance and competency, and criticized severely any solution but his own. When he was asked, "What are you really after?" he cried out, "One person who will love me."

We can heal each other. The love we carry in our hearts is a power, a precious ointment for which others are yearning. So often that power remains unused, and love diminishes among men instead of growing. People suffer a deeper loneliness, a greater frustration, because we forget the gift in us, the gift for others.

We are poor men, we are weak, we are sinners. True, only too true. All our lives our weakness will be there, our personal poverty, our sin. Forever we need daily bread to strengthen us, the power of God and His mercy. Until the time when Christ will be all in all, we will stand in need of such aid. In the meantime, we are never quite free of our faults, and we will never be free of our need for God. As a matter of fact, when Christ finally returns, it will be to take full possession of us, to share fully His life. We will praise God for having nothing of our own, for being totally dependent upon Him.

Having admitted this, that he is a poor man, the Christian begins to discover that a new life stirs in him, a new hope, a new joy, a new power. Christ lives in him. He can act differently, he can change, for the roots of love and unselfishness have taken hold in his depths. He begins to see daily living as a game, the game of love. In every meeting with another person, he knows that the way of life is to play the game, not withdraw from it. Each day he is challenged. The forces of life struggle with the forces of death within his own heart. He can accept or refuse. He can move toward life or away from it. He can live in reality or in partial and total illusion.

In this ping-pong game of giving and receiving, he fails over and over again, he misses the ball. But let him continue to play the game. Let him pick up the ball and send it back.

It takes much faith to believe that love is the very fabric of reality. It takes much courage to keep on loving when so much love is rejected. It takes much hope to believe in happiness when the forces of shame and fear and depression attack us from inside and from outside. "Will there ever be union among men? Will there ever be unity in myself? When will we know peace and be able to rest in each other's love, in the love of Christ which was let loose on Calvary?"

Life is mostly a struggle for hope, vibrant hope in the power of love. The saints had it and they brought comfort and strength to many. We too have it, but perhaps in a dormant or semi-dormant stage. Christ's love is in us, a power that needs only to be exercised.

How great is love, how powerful! We experience it at times. And we've experienced the kind of death that enters our hearts when we refuse to forgive or to give of ourselves. We are all invited to *life*, right now, this very moment. A little story illustrates very well the point I have been trying to make.

A man put on a lavish banquet for his friends. The table was jammed with choice meats, seafood, salads, desserts. But the only available utensils were long spoons set at each place. Some tried to feed themselves, but the spoons were so long that they couldn't get them into their mouths. The others fed each other in a friendly and even playful spirit. Needless to say, these latter were fully satisfied.

May we Christians fully believe in the power of love Christ has given to us. May we seek to serve others, to care for others. Then we will be truly living. We will be crying the Gospel with our lives. We will be affirming to the world that God is indeed alive, that He is the God of the *living*.

The Filled
Don't Need
a Banquet

Yesterday at the Eucharistic Liturgy, I was filled with a great joy of understanding something in a way I had not understood before. The first reading (1 John 3:13-18) in a few sentences brings us a definite revelation: we know Jesus loves us because He laid down His life for us. If He did this, then this is what we must do for each other—not only with words but in action.

My immediate thought on reading this was that at one time in my life I would have tried to understand this passage, and then I would have determined to do this or that for someone, serve them in some way or other. I still think that the reading contains that lesson. However, if one's outlook on the situation is, "I shall now help here, now there," one can easily become a sort of professional do-gooder.

The second reading, the Gospel, seemed to give me a better key to understanding the first lesson. It (Luke 14:16-24) relates the story of the man who invited many people to come to a great dinner. They made excuses. They would not come. So he called in the poor, the crippled, the blind, and the lame. And even after all these came in, there was still room for more. He had his servants force people to come in from every highway and byway.

Hearing this Gospel I got excited. The thing that caused the excitement was real, perhaps God-inspired. It became for me a key to understanding the foregoing message.

The Gospel said to me that those who came to the banquet symbolize the people in this world who are called to be witnesses of Christ. To witness to Christ doesn't demand that we should own some land that needs to be inspected, or five pair of oxen to test, or a new wife to delight in, nor to have anything at all, in fact. How amazing, yet, that this coming to the banquet does require that we be poor, crippled, blind, lame, and half-dragged in by the hand of God, because we are too dense to run the right way when we hear an invitation to a banquet.

That is what witnesses to Christ's presence are. Not because we are gifted, not because we are clever, not because we are beautiful people have we been invited, but because no matter how crummy we are, no matter what hopeless, groping dopes we are, no matter how tattered and shattered we are, no matter how despicable, ridiculous or poor, we have done the one important thing required to witness to Christ: *we have come to the banquet.*

It is the banquet, the bounty, the festivity, the love and warm welcome of our host, His goodness and graciousness and wholehearted acceptance of the poorest crumbs in town — that is what we are witnesses to, His goodness.

That, I think, is what St. John meant in his letter; that is the key to understanding that we are witnesses to Christ not only in word and in deed, but also in simply accepting the invitation to the banquet which witnesses to the Father's generosity. If we have not entered the banquet hall and joined in the festivities wholeheartedly, and become guests of the most gracious host of all creation, then we are in danger of witnessing only to our own pride or foolishness.

It is only in the shocking abyss of our poverty that the banquet may be received. It is only in this that the banquet's good effects will be seen or known. Those who are not hungry don't need a banquet. Even more pitiful are those who hunger and seek satiety elsewhere, not knowing that there is only one banquet and one host to satisfy them.

It is in poverty, in humility, in accepting the truth of who we are that God's glory can shine forth. Without Him we are about as great as an empty hole in the ground, no matter what accomplishments, talents, or performances we manifest. With Him added to our poverty, there can be Christian witness.

It is only His love, the fantastic force of it working within our fragile, dubious framework, that can say to other people and to the world: "See, look, everybody. You are not alone in your sorrow, not alone in your sin, not alone in your suffering, not alone in your despair. See, I have taken from among you these poorest, these most disreputable, most crippled, most blind, most thick-headed, most stubborn.

"I have taken these most sinful, most suffering, most alone, most fearful, most hopeless. See, I make them shine among you, filled with hope and faith and love. If I can do that with these most helpless of the hopeless, then you too can be filled with all my good things. *Come to the banquet!*"

It's Easy
To Be
Cruel

"God forgives, but I don't" — this is a major part of the world's problem. We don't forgive. I don't forgive my brother, he doesn't forgive another brother, who in turn doesn't forgive another brother. Our hearts are suspicious, fearful, hostile, and we lose our happiness. We who have everything we materially need to make us happy are not happy.

No society, no family can last for any length of time without constant forgiveness on the part of each member. We need both to forgive and to ask to be forgiven. We, all of us, are deficient. How often we hurt one another simply by thoughtlessness, by a lack of delicacy.

A friend shares a beautiful event with me. I should jump with joy and shout "Alleluia." But, I'm tired, and so I yawn and say, "Sounds great," instead of praising God with my friend for a beautiful happening. Someone shares a sorrow, but I'm blind to the depths of that sorrow, to the intensity of my brother's pain. I do not help him carry his burden.

Love ought to be a thrilling, challenging thing, always opening on to new vistas, new and more expanded horizons. Every day carries upon its wings exciting opportunities for love, adventure, fresh insights into the reality of God as revealed by people, things, events, and one's own heart. For how many hours or days or weeks am I dead, dead to love, to happiness, because someone has hurt me and I haven't forgiven, I haven't forgotten? I just sit there within myself, licking my wounds, while life passes me by.

We human beings can hurt each other without even trying very hard. It's easy to be hard, to be cruel! Simply by striving to achieve our own security, simply by seeking our own welfare, simply by doing our own thing, we can interfere violently and dreadfully with the good of another in our daily human relationships as well as in society.

Seek your own good, do your own thing, without thought of anybody else and you produce all the fuel necessary for family divisions, class hatreds, national disasters, and international conflagrations. How much we need to be aware of all this! How much we need to ask forgiveness from all men, for we are all guilty of injustice, of seeking our own good at the expense of others.

God forgives, and, please God, I too shall forgive, so that love may be born in families, nations, and the world. Nation must forgive nation; employer, employee; employee, employer; the young, the old; the old, the young; men, women; women, men; the Church, society; society, the Church; children, parents; parents, children.

Love grows in a family, a community, a nation, when each person in it strives to be part of the whole —not dominating but serving, not doing one's own thing, but "our thing." Without forgiveness love dies and happiness evaporates. The reason for this is not hard to discover. Since nobody is perfect, injuries of all kinds will happen. Sometimes the only draw-bridge left to link one person to another is the draw-bridge of mercy and forgiveness.

When all other bridges have collapsed, that bridge can always be erected. That is why there is something divine about it, something so soothing and healing. Forgiveness is one of the most beau-tiful expressions of the power of love.

Love
Yourself
as Your
Neighbor

God loved us first. Let us love Him back by serving our neighbor. This is a simple, clear, unequivocal statement, a clear objective for each day, a definite challenge. But in the process of trying to love others by service, we often bog down. We quickly reach a limit. We find the service easy enough, but the neighbor difficult at times.

Often the closer the relationship the more do we experience the difficulties. Ask any husband and wife. Ask any community of religious. Ask anyone even from among groups of laity who have come together specifically to live the Gospel. Strangers affect us less than our intimate associates, perhaps because they matter less to us.

We want to love, but we find it difficult. Why? There are many reasons. We Christians are, after all, engaged in a warfare. Christ has chosen our weakness with which to build His Body and to spread His kingdom. This task involves a lasting struggle against all those things which try to pull us in the direction of complete egoism. And we cannot help feeling this struggle deeply, for the forces of good and evil have chosen our very being as the battle-field. Such is the condition of man and we are all subject to it. And since love of God expressed in serv-ice to the neighbor is of the essence of Christianity, let us not be surprised if some of the greatest tests come in this area.

Christ *did* say to love our enemies. This also means to love anyone who hurts us: a wife, a husband, an associate. When we are hurt, our love weakens. We strike back or we experience resentments, fol-lowed by guilt feelings and self-punishment.

If we cannot forgive our enemies, it may be because we cannot forgive ourselves. If we cannot accept others as they are, it may be because we can-not accept ourselves as we are. If we cannot love our neighbor, it may be because we do not love ourselves.

Let us look at this matter of proper self-love. Don't all the spiritual books condemn most violently all manner of self-love? Didn't St. Augustine label it the arch-enemy of the City of God? Isn't selfish-ness at the root of all vices? Yes, certainly — but let's make a few distinctions.

Christ commands us to love our neighbor *as ourselves*. There must be, therefore, a holy form of self-love. To seek one's happiness outside the order established by God is evil self-love, the source of all sin of which the saints speak. But to seek one's perfection and happiness within that order is proper self-love. For truly, God wants us to be happy. That is why He made us.

The saints were happy people, even though they suffered much. Listen to your own heart and every beat will tell you that you want desperately to be happy. The great philosophers teach us that. They say that our whole nature tends of necessity in the direction of seeking happiness and fulfillment. The right to the pursuit of happiness has been enshrined in the civil documents of many a nation.

We want to be happy. We have no choice in the matter. We can choose, for better or for worse, the means to happiness. Some paths lead to it, some paths create greater misery. Some choices bring us to God who alone can satisfy our longings; others tend to separate us from Him. To seek union with God is to seek happiness where it can be found and to have the proper kind of self-love.

The saint is the one who really takes good care of himself. He appreciates himself. He knows his own value, his own worth, and the love that went into his making and remaking by Christ. He has proper self-love when he denies himself in the service of others, when he fasts and prays, trusts and loves. He loses his life to save it. He forgets himself and thinks of others.

The sinner in reality despises himself. He does not provide good things for himself. Greed corrupts everything he touches. Power, privilege, pleasure, sought after for what they will give him, quickly disappoint, disturb, and frustrate. He wants to save his life, and Wisdom tells us quite plainly that that is the best way to lose it. He does not appreciate himself at his true value. He gives himself fodder and refuses the caviar of the wedding feast. He does not truly love himself. He is merely selfish.

The saint loves himself. He wants the best for himself. He also wants the best for his neighbor. He loves his neighbor as himself. He comes to realize that these two goods are bound up together. His

life becomes one of service to those around him and
to the world. Love of God and neighbor are one love
and cannot be separated.

Now many of us who want to love God and neighbor often fail miserably because we don't love
ourselves properly. We can't quite believe that
God is really anxious to help us. We see our faults,
our weaknesses. We try to improve, with little
success. Shame lives in our hearts. We too despise
ourselves. We're so annoyed with ourselves, and so
we are often annoyed with others. Having little
patience with ourselves, we are tempted to have
little patience with others. Having little mercy with
ourselves, we are merciless towards others.

Self-acceptance is essential to a healthy, happy,
and holy life. We are commanded to love all of God's
creation. We ourselves are part of that creation!
When God made us He made a good thing. Why not
love that poor good thing? Unless we do, we rob
God of glory. We refuse to acknowledge the magnificence of His handiwork. We are unable to appreciate
the other good things He has made because we do
not appreciate that part of creation closest of all—
ourselves.

No, we are not as good as we often think we are.
We know the meanness of which we are capable.
But we are greater than we are willing to admit.
We have gifts of mind and body that we have scarcely
begun to use, not to mention the very life of Christ
in us. Our potential for good is far greater than we
imagine. Often it lies dormant because we do not love
ourselves as we ought.

Which Winds Will Prevail?

Winds. Winds blowing over mankind. Two kinds of winds. The wild winds of hatred and confusion, howling, unruly, destructive. Winds scattering seeds of death. The strong and gentle winds of love, of peace, of openness, orderly, soothing, calming. Winds nourishing life.

Which winds will be the prevailing ones? The winds of simplicity or confusion, warm winds or cold winds? Which will prevail in you and in me?

I carry within myself both seeds of destruction and seeds of life for winds to scatter about. Which kind of harvest will be reaped this year, this very day?

In his "Hymn for the Church Militant," G. K. Chesterton speaks sane and strong words to all Christians and men of good will everywhere:

> Great God, that bowest sky and star,
> Bow down our towering thoughts to Thee,
> And grant us in a faltering war
> The firm feet of humility.
>
> Lord, we that snatch the swords of flame,
> Lord, we that cry about Thy ear,

70

We too are weak with pride and shame,
We too are as our foemen are.

Yea, we are mad as they are mad,
Yea, we are blind as they are blind,
Yea, we are very sick and sad
Who bring good news to all mankind.

The dreadful joy Thy Son has sent
Is heavier than any care;
We find, as Cain his punishment,
Our pardon more than we can bear.

Lord, when we cry Thee far and near
And thunder through all lands unknown
The Gospel into every ear,
Lord, let us not forget our own.

Cleanse us from ire of creed or class,
The anger of the idle kings;
Sow in our souls, like living grass,
The laughter of all lowly things.

"Bow down our towering thoughts to Thee" so
that we may appreciate, understand and live the
simple, direct, and uncompromising message of the
Gospel: Love your enemies. Judge not. Seek and
you shall find. Don't be anxious; your Father knows
that you need all these things. Seek the kingdom of
God first. Love one another as I have loved you. Abide
in my love. The Spirit of truth will live with you and
be in you. Simple words, but powerful, strengthening,
and full of light.

We are apt to be very rational people. We need
to learn how to bow down our towering thoughts to
God. We believe that revelation is full of mystery
before which every believer must bow his head. But
we are much more inclined to begin with reason and

end with reason even in matters of faith. To have the winds of grace bring forth within us the seeds of life, we need to acquire more of the faith approach to the mysteries of Christ.

May the Holy Spirit, who is the power of love and the strong wind and breath of God, break open our hearts and fashion in each of us a heart of flesh, a warm heart, an open heart, that His wind may blow through us and into a stormy world.

The
Jesus
Prayer

"Lord Jesus Christ, Son of the living God, be merciful to me a sinner." Over the years, this prayer has become for many people almost a way of life, a way of responding to Christ's injunction to pray always. Popularized as "The Jesus Prayer," it is also known in the Eastern Church as the "Prayer of the Heart."

A fine little book, *The Way of the Pilgrim,* written nearly a hundred years ago by an anonymous peasant, tells how this man travelled all over Russia seeking someone who would teach him how to pray always. After much traveling and many adventures he meets a Russian holy man, a "staretz," who instructs him.

"The Jesus Prayer," he said, "has two parts. The first—Lord Jesus Christ, Son of the living God—leads our thoughts to the life of Jesus Christ. It summarizes the whole Gospel."

And indeed it does. For Jesus appears in the Gospel as Lord and Savior. He has come to save.

And save He does, through His healing and teaching activities, through His passion, death, and resurrection. He is Lord, powerful head of all creation, ruler, the union between God and man. His love streams forth from Calvary and reaches out to every man, to heal, to save, to strengthen and transform.

"The second part of the Jesus prayer—have mercy on me, a sinner—brings us face to face with the fact of our own helplessness and sinfulness. It is to be noted that the desire of a poor, sinful, humble soul could not be put into words more wise, more clear cut, more exact than these—'have mercy on me.' No other form of words would be as satisfying and full as this.

"'Have mercy on me' means not only the desire for pardon arising from fear, but is the sincere cry of filial love, which puts its hope in the mercy of God and humbly acknowledges it is too weak to break its own will and to keep a watchful guard over itself in the gift of strength from God, to enable us to resist temptation and overcome our sinful inclinations. It is like a penniless debtor asking his kindly creditor not only to forgive him the debt but also to pity his extreme poverty and to give him alms. That is what these profound words 'have mercy on me' express.

"It is like saying: 'Gracious Lord, forgive me my sins and help me to put myself right; arouse in my soul a strong impulse to follow Your bidding. Bestow Your grace in forgiving my actual sins and in turning my heedless mind, will and heart to You alone.'"

The Jesus prayer establishes us in the truth. It brings us back to reality. It puts us in a proper relationship with God. We are sinners in need of salvation. We are incomplete, in need of fulfillment. The Jesus prayer brings to us immediately the power of God's love. At that moment God does forgive our sins.

"Prayer," says St. John Chrysostom, although we are full of sin when we utter it, immediately cleanses us. God's loving kindness to us is great, yet we sinners are listless, are not willing to give even one small hour to God in thanksgiving and barter the time of prayer—which is more important than anything—for the hustle and cares of living, forgetting God and our duty. For that reason we often meet with misfortunes and calamities; yet even these the all-loving providence of God uses for our instruction and to turn our hearts to Him."

This Jesus prayer is also called the Prayer of the Heart because through its constant repetition it becomes synchronized with our own heartbeats.

Let us often say the Jesus prayer. May it become truly the prayer of our heart, and we shall live unceasingly in the power of God's merciful love.

Christst
Our
Healing

In St. Luke's Gospel, we read: "When he [Jesus] had finished speaking he said to Simon, 'Put out into deep water and lower your nets for a catch.' Simon answered, 'Master, we have been hard at it all night long and have caught nothing; but if you say so, I will lower the nets.' Upon doing this they caught such a great number of fish their nets were at the breaking point" (Lk. 5:4-6).

When I was ordained thirty-three years ago I knew that the life of a priest wasn't an easy one. But I never expected it to be filled with such amazing and wonderful things. God often does such things through the hands of a priest. I have seen with my own eyes the miraculous catch of fish that so surprised Simon and the other apostles. These words of Jesus Christ are valid and true.

Despite appearances to the contrary, I firmly believe that they are coming true for many people in many parts of the world. Certainly there is a growing awareness of the oneness of the human race, a greater search for unity, a deeper seeking for God, for meaning, for life, for love and freedom. We Christians alive today are privileged to bear within our own hearts and minds and hands the power and the love of Jesus Christ.

Christ is alive. He lives among us. He does amazing things. Each one of us experiences darkness. We experience in our hearts the anguish, the doubts, and the fears of all men. Often we don't know exactly what God expects of us next, but we know that the Lord is our light. The Lord Jesus is our lover and the source of all the love that we need to receive and give.

We seek, we search, we study, we attend innumerable courses and lectures. All this is very fine. But there comes a point in our lives where we find no more answers in the studies and courses. The answer we seek is not to be found in a sentence, a course, a book. The answer is Jesus Christ, the Lord, the Person of Christ Himself. And it is the Spirit who reveals Jesus to us as Someone, a living person who desires a very unique and personal relationship with me and with every man.

The Lord is our light, our healing, and our salvation, and He continues to be our light and healing and salvation from day to day, from moment to moment. St. John says that the Light came into the world. This must mean that we lived in the darkness. Should we be surprised when we find ourselves in darkness? If He is the way, it must be true that we have lost our way. Should it surprise us that we wander aimlessly about sometimes? If He is the truth, it must be true that we are enveloped by much falsity about ourselves. Should it surprise us if our minds are confused about life?

Christ is, He acts, His words are life-giving. He tells us to listen, to pay attention, then act on

His word. Each time we act on this word in faith, something deep and powerful comes alive within us. And something comes alive, not only inside of us, but inside others, inside the whole universe.

The human race is one. We are a community. With all our differences and hostilities, we long for one community. We experience the pain of being limited and divided within ourselves. Christ gave no deep explanation of pain or the problem of evil. He didn't explain it away; He lived with a great deal of it Himself. So, when we get hurt He says, "I got hurt too and I suffer with you." He shares it and He heals it at its core when He says, "You may go in peace, your sins are forgiven."

Through this process grows a deep understanding of reality, of oneself, of others. We enter into an ocean of love. We come to know that God is love and that He is present in all the moments and events of time.

The Lord Jesus is a real person. He is our life. From Him comes healing and life and love. Let us live in His love at this momentous time in history. Let us give ourselves to this glorious task: the service of others, the building of a better, more peaceful world.

Impossible
Demands
of Christ

"This means that if anyone is in Christ, he has a new creation. The old order has passed away; now all is new!" (2 Cor. 5:17) When anyone is united to Christ he is a new creature. His old life is over and a new life has already begun. The risen Christ lives in him, and the power of His love moves him to live no longer for himself. The Spirit of Christ moves him *to live for him who for their sake died and was raised to life,* and to live for others. Christ "laid down his life for us; we too must lay down our lives for our brothers" (1 Jn. 3:16). A tall order! An impossible order! It can only be possible through the power of the Risen Christ.

Instinctively everything in us rebels, recoils and shrinks from any kind of death, and especially from this death of living for others. In moments of clarity —when we see what is asked of us—we want to run away, to hide, to forget. Our own immense hunger rises to the surface to overwhelm us, our own immense need of healing and of love seems to take priority. Prostrate before the Lord we ask: "How can I feed others who am so hungry myself? How can I heal and be full of compassion, I who am so conscious of my own sickness? How can the emptiness which I am, bring fulfillment to another?"

Paradoxes. Mysteries. And the clear voice of Christ continues to pierce our hearts like a sword: *The man who loses his life shall find it.... Abide in my love.... I am with you until the end of time.* It is in the very experience of our weakness that we come to know the healing power of the living Christ, that we experience His presence, His activity, our union with Him, the depth of our union. St. Paul once said that he rejoiced in the very things which were his weakness, and that then the power of Christ came and rested on him. As the glory of God rested upon the ark in the midst of the raging temptations of the chosen people's wanderings, so will God's presence rest upon us in the midst of trials.

Empty of self and full of Christ, the Christian can do wondrous things. He brings healing, love, compassion to others. His own hunger remains unsatisfied most of the time, and yet he knows that he is being fed, sustained, strengthened, mysteriously in the depths of his being. "He gives to his beloved in sleep" (Ps. 127:2).

United with Christ he is a new creation. He belongs to a new breed of men, even though he must often walk in a new and unfamiliar country. The old, familiar landmarks have disappeared, and no signposts guide his path. Led by the Spirit of the Lord, unmoored and freed from his previous securities, the Christian passes from the valley of desolation to the mountain-tops of hope. Over and over again, he passes from an unbearable awareness of his weakness to a thrilling experience of his union with Christ.

The Christian knows that Christ is alive, that he and Christ are one. He sees reality with new eyes, a vision enlightened by the power of the Risen Christ. Thus a great compassion wells up in his heart for all things and for all men.

Who God is he knows only in mystery, and in his twilight stutters that God is love, God is light, God is power, God is Father of our Lord Jesus Christ. God's ways — how He works among men — he hardly knows. He learns to listen to the Spirit, to test all spirits, to be silent in the presence of the awesome One. Always he lives in a partial mystery, receiving light and strength for the next step of the journey. He becomes like a trusting little child who holds his father's hand and follows, follows, follows.

Great is our God, the Father of our Lord Jesus Christ! Great is the power of His love in which we live and breathe and have our very being.

Loneliness as the Cry of God Within

As we enter into a new era of history, we Christians remember that our whole life in all its aspects is meant to be a service to our brothers and sisters in this world. We have a work to do for the person next to us, for our next door neighbor, for the people of Pakistan, India, Brazil, the United States, Canada, China—the whole world.

Our service has been classified and labeled, among other things, "the works of mercy," whereby Christians shower their love upon their brothers and sisters. But the "work" I want to call attention to right now is of a different sort. It is one that will benefit those who do not know that man is meant for God.

Now very often this particular work of ours is mistakenly called loneliness—a very dreadful word in our vocabulary. We know the feeling of loneliness. We know the state of loneliness. There are times when it seems immensely difficult, if not impossible, to communicate with God or with any other human being. We feel very much separated, very much alone, very much contained within our own little world, our own little prison.

There is, of course, an evil kind of loneliness, born of arrogance, mistrust, and pride. There is a psychological loneliness which comes from illusory feelings of rejection and which can be cured. The loneliness I mean now is the one which every Christian who thinks and prays, who believes in God, who wants to love his brothers, has to endure sooner or later. It is the discovery of what I think is the greatest insight into ourselves, into what it means to be human. It takes thought and prayer and love to arrive at that kind of loneliness. It develops best in a loving community.

Loneliness of this type isn't an evil, but rather a beautiful thing. *It is a human being knowing that he is made for God and longing for the coming of God to him and to the whole world.*

So what is this state of loneliness? It is a mature realization that we are made for something greater than any human being. We are made for something greater than friendship among men, greater than any human achievement, greater than any kind of personal success. We come to realize that we are made for God!

When the Christian experiences loneliness, it is really the Holy Spirit in his heart, calling him, revealing to him that there is within him an enclosed garden where God lives. It is the Spirit saying, "You are running all over the world in your heart and mind's eye. Your desires are on the rampage. Now stop that! Drop your desires. Be quiet. Stand still. Float down within yourself until you rest in me."

Whenever we experience loneliness, let us remember that it should be one of the most important experiences in our lives. It is a call from the Spirit to meet the Trinity in the depths of our hearts. As you enter into this enclosed garden you will understand what it is to be alone with the Alone, and how all loneliness is ultimately conquered.

Say to God: "My soul thirsts for You." No matter how alone we may feel, how alone we may actually be, God will be there. He will come quickly and allow us to rest in His presence and in His love.

The Extraordinary Ordinary

Many feel that they are wasting their lives, that their work is unimportant and their contribution to Christ's saving act just about nil. Their motto seems to be that of the defeatist: "I hope not to do too much harm before I die."

True enough, the vast majority of us are called by God all through life to do little things, unimportant things. To get up in the morning to another day of lifting, carrying, washing, cooking, cleaning, painting, hammering, teaching, nursing—repeating over and over again for years on end the same mechanical gestures.

Our eye is not clear and we judge by the standards of worldly prudence. We feel unimportant perhaps because we would like to be important in the eyes of the world; we want to do something startling that will make others sit up and take notice; we want to be made to feel important. Many say: "My life is useless," "I'm only a housewife," "I'm just a farmer, or carpenter, or factory worker or clerk," not realizing sufficiently that the infinite God Himself was "just a carpenter," that our Lady was "only a housewife," that St. Joseph never did anything startling in a worldly sense.

How beneficial to look at the Holy Family of Nazareth on those days when dissatisfaction with the ordinariness of daily living takes hold of us. The three most important people ever to exist—all doing little things! Here perfect worship was rendered to God. Here redemption was begun. Here every act was clothed with grandeur because of love— love incarnate in the midst of mankind, received from above and given back in perfection, each moment filled with its full measure of faith, trust, and love: a perfect circle, a constant movement, a wild activity so intense that it passed unnoticed, as motionless as a fast moving wheel.

All of us are called to repeat daily the most important actions ever performed, to use our hands as Christ and Mary and Joseph used them, making gestures infinitely sanctified. They are made holy, precious, redemptive by the One who made them in Galilee thousands of years after He had decreed from all time that they should be the lot of man. Wisdom decreed them then, and love accomplished them later, that we might touch and see what God considers important, what *is* important and what is not.

There are many ways of sweeping a floor or piling wood or doing anything indifferent in itself: a pagan way, an evil way, a mediocre way, a redemptive way. It all depends on the intention, on the love in the heart of the doer.

At Fatima our Lady told us to do penance and she specified the penance: doing little things well. With prayer, she added, this would save the world. Done with love it will set the world on fire. For such is the power of love, of that *caritas* we call divine grace, that it does transform ordinariness into extraordinariness, unimportance into greatest importance, little things into big things. A few years ago Benny Goodman popularized a one-line tune: "It isn't what you do, it's the way you do it." It's a good line. Let's make it ours.

What is great? To do the will of the Father irrespective of the form which it takes in various lives. In this is joy, in this one finds the redemptive cross, in this fulfillment, and unsurpassable greatness, the greatness of a beloved son of a loving Father. Such is the power of little things done out of great love.

So let us rejoice that our lives are useful, valuable, redemptive, important. Let us rejoice that we are small and weak and unimportant in the eyes of the world. Let us rejoice at our needs and our inability to fulfill them, for we have a Father who takes care of all the needs of His little ones. We have a Father who reveals His secrets to little children and to adults who have become as little children, a Father who insists on using *those whom the world considers absurd to shame the wise; he singled out the weak of this world to shame the strong* (cf. 1 Cor. 1:19). We have a Father like no other father.

A day spent in doing little things with love is a day well spent. A person can go to bed in peace. The Father has been well served, well loved, and He is well pleased.

We Have a Loving Father

       The Child once born in a manger came to complete, in His person, actions, and words, the continuing revelation of God to man. As St. Paul puts it in the opening words of the letter to the Hebrews: "In times past, God spoke in fragmentary and varied ways to our fathers through the prophets; in this the final age he has spoken to us through his Son, whom he has made heir of all things and through whom he first created the universe. This Son is the reflection of the Father's glory, the exact representation of the Father's being, and he sustains all things by his powerful word. When he had cleansed us from our sins, he took his seat at the right hand of the Majesty in heaven" (Heb. 1:1-4).

  Christ comes with a message, a gospel, with good news. Thousands of holy men and women, thousands of holy and learned theologians, have discussed and analyzed this message. Many people in our own day ask: "Is it possible to live the Gospel today?" For most of us, I think it is difficult if not impossible to apply directly to our own lives every counsel or pre-scription of the Gospel. Most of us would have to think twice about taking Christ's injunction to His disciples, "Provide yourselves with neither gold nor silver nor copper in your belts; no traveling bag, no change of shirt, no sandals, no walking staff" (Mt. 10:9-10). Some of the saints did—but not all.

Yes, there can be much discussion, many opin-ions concerning similar prescriptions in the New Testament. So much depends upon the individual Christian's personal circumstances. But the essence of Christ's message applies to all, and in this sense we can answer a very definite "yes" to the question "Is it possible to live the Gospel today?"

Many books have been written, many discussions have taken place over the interpretation of this or that statement of Christ. But one thing is absolutely sure, clear, unambiguous, which all can live no matter what state or status or age they happen to be in: *You have a Father...be not anxious...do His will today.*

You have a Father. Fatherhood implies origin, beginnings. A father is one who brings another to life. God is our Father. We come from Him. Our soul came directly from His creative hand. Our body comes from Him through our parents for He gave them the power to co-create that body with Him. The glorious new life—a share of His own—received at Baptism, comes from Him. He is in truth our Father, our Origin and Beginning. All fatherhood proceeds from Him.

He loves us. So very much does He care for our true well-being that He sent His beloved Son to be one of us. He wills and accepts the excruciating sacrifice of this most tenderly loved Son. He makes Him our Head, the Head of a new Being, a new Body. He makes us one with Him.

True, He lays down certain laws that we must observe. But they have a single purpose: to make one a loving person, to eliminate the obstacles to love, to unite us ever more intimately with Love. He prepares us for heaven. But pain comes into our lives and we are tempted to doubt His love and to question His care. We find our desires unfulfilled. This has to be. Each one of us has to struggle with his self-love so as to become loving. Each one of us has to learn to give of himself so as to be ready for heaven. Perfect joy reigns there because each person gives himself fully to the others and receives fully from the others. The struggle against self-love upon earth prepares for the perfect, loving, ecstatic communication of heaven.

Christ tells us that we have a Father, that we should not be anxious, that we should seek to do His lovable will today. He will teach us love. His message is bad news to our self-love. His message is good news to our inner spirit, for it means that God has made us for far more than we could ever imagine. He has made us for true and perfect love.

It is possible to live the Gospel today. It is possible for all. We have a Father who takes care of all our needs. We have nothing to be anxious about. Let us love Him in return by doing His holy will today.

Live
Like a
Creature

At certain times of the year we think of making resolutions, of changing what needs to be changed in us. We think of improvement. I suggest a very simple, all-embracing resolution: live as a creature each day!

That is a simple resolution, but one unusually deep, unusually fruitful, if we live it in the concrete circumstances of each day.

A creature is nothing and has nothing which has not been given to it. Its existence is given moment by moment by the *One* who is Existence. Body and soul come to us from God. Senses, mind, will, emotions, operate only with His cooperation. *Without me you can do nothing* — nothing in the supernatural order, and nothing in the natural order without Him. I cannot flick an eyelid, call out to a friend or move my little finger without God's assistance. Whether I am aware of it or not, my dependence on God is total and constant.

We believe in the Creator, but do we act as creatures? Do we trust *God* or ourselves? Are we *humble* (that is to say truthful), or proud (that is, deceitful), about who we really are? Are we grateful for *His* gifts, or do we attribute them to *ourselves?* Do we live dependent on *His* will, or on *our own?*

Let us resolve to be what we are — creatures. We are creatures who are also beloved sons and daughters of a lavish, loving Father. If we seem to receive little of that love, let us not blame God. He gives, ever gives to those who wish to receive. He fills them with His life, His grace, His strength, His unselfishness, His love. They become merciful as He is merciful. They become gentle even as Christ is meek and humble. They choose the road of pain to be with Christ, their Beloved. His peace permeates their whole beings, a peace which no one can take from them. And His joy shines forth. Yes, the Bible, the writings of the early Fathers of the Church, the lives of the saints — all testify to God's lavish love.

How explain the present immense problems of our world except to say that men refuse to be what they are, creatures? Men think they are gods, self-sufficient, independent, capable "of running their own show." And so often we do the same with respect to our personal difficulties and activities. If we believe in the Creator, let us live that belief. Let us act as creatures.

Let us start at the beginning, and the beginning is Mary, the one human being who knew herself to be a creature, fully a creature. Mary knew this as a little child knows her dependence. She spoke to God as a creature. She said *fiat*. . .do with me as you please. That word made her the Mother of the Savior.

Fiat is the greatest word we can speak! It contains our whole being. When we say it, we speak the truth and live in the truth. We come to rest in our proper place, the hand of God.

For this have we been created and redeemed. For this have we been endowed with the glorious faculties of mind and will — to say *"Fiat*...do with me as you please...I am your child and You are my God."

We want to do great things, to fulfill ourselves, to surpass ourselves. We dream of success and achievement. This dream can be realized. High achievement is possible. All we need do is say *fiat,* and live it, in our thoughts, work, and play, in all our relationships with others. *Fiat* perfectly expresses all that we are. It is our word. In it we express ourselves.

We want so much to be ourselves, to express ourselves, to fulfill ourselves. We try to achieve this in so many ways—by competing with our neighbors, by seeking to impress others, by yearning for prestige, status, high position. And yet all these desires can be satisfied. The secret of success, true success, has been revealed in Mary's *fiat.*

Let us start at the beginning, and the beginning is Mary. Her *fiat* will cleanse our proud hearts. Her example will encourage us to speak the one word that matters—*fiat.* Her love makes it possible for us to live as creatures because she brought Christ to us. She is full of grace, full of love. She is our spiritual Mother. Once, through the power of the Holy Spirit, she conceived and brought Christ into the world. Eagerly she waits, anxious to conceive Him again and bring Him to birth in us and in our world.

But even as God Himself waited upon her *fiat* before He would come to us, so also her activity is limited by our receptivity. Who will say *fiat* to the Mother of God? Who will imitate her, the perfect creature? In whom will she be able to conceive Christ? Who will accept her love?

Two thousand years ago a girl allowed God to lavish His gifts upon her. She allowed God to do His will and the world was redeemed. Who will say *fiat* to Mary? Who will be channels of her love? Who will allow the power of her love to fill them and the earth?

Our
Family
Album

God, who is love, has constantly attempted to fashion men into one family, a family bound together by love. The Bible reveals this purpose.

Beginning with Abraham, we find God preparing mankind for union with one another in Christ through the Church. To Abraham He says: "Go forth from the land of your kinsfolk and from your father's house to a land that I will show you. I will make of you a great nation" (Gn. 12:1-2). He chose Abraham to be the father of the faithful, of those who believe and trust in God, of those who want to join His family.

Years later, He spoke with another man, Moses. He trained him, purified him, and entrusted to him the shaping of Israel into a holy nation, the people of God. Solemnly, at the foot of Mount Sinai, God established the covenant between Himself and His people: "You have seen for yourselves how I treated the Egyptians and how I bore you up on eagle wings and brought you here to myself. Therefore, if you harken to my voice and keep my covenant, you shall be my special possession.... You shall be to me a kingdom of priests, a holy nation" (Ex. 19:4-6).

Moses, the greatest of the prophets (a prophet is one who speaks for God), trained the Jewish people in the desert. He gave them laws for worship and for moral behavior. He gave them a civil code. Repeatedly he impressed upon them that they had been chosen by God. Repeatedly God manifested His special care for them so that when they entered the promised land they had become a much more cohesive nation.

The history of Israel can be portrayed as a series of cycles. The Jews reject the true God for false gods. They suffer at the hands of their enemies; a prophet appears to tell them of their sin; they do penance, they pray, they return to God, and He saves them from the hands of their enemies. Faithfully God strives to make of them His people.

Some 600 years before Christ they are taken into captivity, into Babylon, a captivity which lasts some forty years. During that time the great prophet Ezekiel reminds them of God's promises, and trains them especially to become now a priestly people. Their bond of unity when they return will be the liturgical services, and, until the time of Christ, the Temple, the Law of God, the promises of God, constitute the main elements of the life of Israel.

Christ comes, Emmanuel, God is now with us, one of us. The union prophesied and developed throughout many centuries now reaches a fulfillment undreamed of by the saints of the Old Testament. True enough, Hosea had spoken about the mystical wedding between God and His people; the Canticle of Canticles had portrayed God as a lover and each man as His beloved. But with Christ, man is invited to share community of life with God.

Christ is the vine, we are the branches. St. Peter calls us a temple of living stones. St. Paul describes our union with God and with one another in terms of the body: "He likewise predestined us through Jesus Christ to be his adopted sons—such was his will and pleasure..." (Eph. 1:5). "The plan he was pleased to decree in Christ, to be carried out in the fullness of time: namely, to bring all things in the heavens and on earth into one under Christ's headship" (Eph. 1:9-10). "He has put all things under Christ's feet and has made him thus exalted, head of the church, which is his body: the fullness of him who fills all the universe in all its parts" (Eph. 1:22). Truly we are citizens with the saints and members of God's household!

What is the Church? It is the family of God, a means of union between all men, a community fashioned by God for Himself and to which all men are called. Union is God's purpose. He takes the initiative, He calls us, He wills this union. Why are we so slow to respond to His love and to submit fully and totally to His lovable will? Eagerly He desires a relationship of love. Clearly He shows His love. Always and forever He forgives the vilest disloyalties. And yet we hesitate, we don't quite believe, we don't quite trust Him. He invites. We respond half-heartedly or not at all. Why this refusal to believe in love, to believe that we are made for love, to believe in God's plan for our happiness?

Never was a Lover more persistent, more unselfish, more loyal. Never was the proposed love affair more thrilling, more satisfying, more enjoyable. Never was the pursued more unworthy. When shall we believe in the power of His love?

Citizen of Two Worlds

The Christian belongs to two societies. He is a member of secular society, of a town or city, of a certain nation. The people of a given city work together to satisfy each other's needs—the need for food, clothing, shelter, education, recreation, friendship. They contribute toward making the world a "better place to live in." At least, that is the plan of God for man in his relationship to other men who form what is known as "secular society." Each needs the others. The farmer needs the doctor and the doctor needs the farmer. The consumer needs the producer and the producer needs the consumer. Capital needs labor and labor needs capital. The needs of all must be provided for by all. Serious trouble develops in a city or a country when a group of people care only for their own interests.

The Christian is also a member of the Church, of Christ's Body, a society which exists to unite men to God and with one another. How exactly will Christians unite men to God through Christ? What will be their program and approach?

One approach has been to set up places of worship wherever possible. Yes, all agree on this. The local community should have a place where its members can worship the Lord and receive instruction in their beliefs.

Another way has been to develop institutions such as schools, hospitals, facilities for the distribution of Christian literature. Until recently, the vast majority of Christians has given its nod of approval to such projects. Such a movement began in the fourth century when, under Constantine, Church and State, the temporal and the spiritual, became so intermingled as often to be indistinguishable.

Today, society has become almost totally secular. The Church exercises its influence over fewer and fewer institutions.

The Church has been rejected in some localities, and churchmen may resent the rejection. Some of the Church's cherished institutions are taken away from her, sometimes violently, sometimes by force of circumstances, sometimes unjustly.

Faced with these profound changes, the Church is reassessing and re-examining the essential values and the essential mission which Christ entrusted to her. What exactly is her role and the role of the committed Christian in today's world?

What is the role of the Church if not to form Christians who will witness to Christ in society, and spread His message of peace and love to others? Did not Christ say, *You are the leaven in the dough?* He did not say,"You are the whole batch of dough." He also said, "My kingdom does not belong to this world" (Jn. 18:36).

Christians are to do the work of Christ, the work for which Christ established His Church. They are to join hands with men of other faiths, or of no faith, and, shoulder to shoulder, help truly to make the world a better place. The Christian should bring to this immense task his Christian love nourished by the faith-community to which he belongs.

Without the element of Christian love, society can indeed be built—but there is a strong possibility of it growing into a monstrosity. It is the glorious task of the Christian to be the leaven in secular society which, under the direction and power of the Spirit of Love, can penetrate the whole mass.

All
Together
Now

We desire communication, understanding, union. Witness the growth of ecumenism over the last fifty years. Witness the United Nations. Consider how prevalent the word "dialogue" has become in our thinking and conversation. Nations strain after union.

In the Church, the doctrine of the Body of Christ stands out more clearly than it did when St. Paul wrote to the first Christians. Today we know Christ is our Head. We know we are members of one another. We know the interdependence of the body's various organs. Baptism, Confirmation, Holy Orders make of all Christians a royal priesthood varying in degree of power in the Body of Christ.

In the area of priest-people relations, we are being challenged with the realization of a new developing relationship being brought into being by the Spirit of Christ. Priests and people are becoming more aware of their interdependence, and the walls which separate the ordained from the laity, the sanctuary from the nave, the governing from the governed, are crumbling.

The Second Vatican Council had, for one of its objectives, the clarification of the layman's role, his

place in the Church. Laymen have cried, and they
continue to cry, the Gospel with their lives, to be
witnesses of the resurrection, to bring God's love to
other men, to spread the kingdom in preparation for
the parousia. Clearly, in our day, the Holy Spirit desires with a great desire that all members of Christ's
Body be agents of His will.

On a day-to-day, practical level, priests and
people are attempting to cooperate in assisting the
coming of the kingdom. They are cooperating in various enterprises, discovering one another as chosen
members of one body, each with his own personal
talents, graces, and functions. The dialogue has
more than begun. Over the past few decades priests
and laity have been learning from one another. This
is a very marvelous and admirable development in
our day.

But immediately a danger arises: our innate tendency to consider one another merely as human beings, to judge from natural standards, to be attracted
by natural qualities or repelled by natural defects.
Our relationship must be built first and foremost on
faith. Let lay people believe in the priesthood of
Christ shared by the ordained ministry. Let priests
believe in the priesthood of Christ shared by the ordained ministry. Let priests believe in the laity's
Baptism and Confirmation. In a relationship so sacred,
so holy, so powerful, faith must prevail, for it is Christ
who dwells in each, who has transformed each into
Himself and who exercises His power in each according to His will.

Human beings are prone to say "I like," or "I
don't like." They are wont to be attracted to one
another because of a pleasing personality, good looks,
good manners, education, and the like. So often we
hear these personal preferences of laity and clergy

alike for one another. Great faith is required from all. We must believe in one another. How often have apostolic projects been killed or hampered because of lack of faith, because of natural·antipathy, because of jealousy? How often has the Holy Spirit been "grieved" simply because we rejected His instruments?

Humility is needed also, I mean a deep, constant, and practical appreciation of our personal poverty. Whether we be priests or the laity, we are nothing of ourselves and we have nothing. We are beings totally dependent for our continued existence — for our next breath — upon the only One who gives existence.

When Christians meet to plan the growth of the kingdom, only one question should be asked: What does the Spirit of Christ want of us today? Sometimes the answer will come from the clergy, sometimes it will come from the laity, sometimes from the honest dialogue between them. The Spirit blows where He wills when Christians gather. If we are aware of our·personal poverty, we will hear His voice when He speaks through another. We will rejoice that He has once again revealed His mysteries, not to the wise and prudent, but to the "anawim," the poor ones, the little ones.

We priests must listen carefully when we meet with lay people to discuss problems and solutions. For years we have been doing all the talking! Our task very often consists in discerning His voice among the numerous voices spoken at a gathering. We are discerners of His activity in others as well as trying to be good teachers ourselves. Let us listen more attentively when we converse. When we gather with our people, let us believe that they have the Holy Spirit also!

Changing
the World
Begins
With Me

Christianity remains sterile until it is practiced. To be effective, the tremendous truths Christ taught must guide, direct, and impregnate the daily actions of men. His words are not only to be learned, but to be lived. "Whoever *does* the will of my heavenly Father, is brother and sister and mother to me" (Mt. 12:50). To do the will of God right now—that's what matters, that's what makes Christianity a living thing, that's what makes all the difference in the world. But it isn't always easy. It requires vigilance, self-control, openness of mind and heart. It requires trust in God and dependence upon His grace, His strength, His love.

The loyal Christian is daily engaged in a struggle as well as a love affair. For daily demands are made upon his love by events and circumstances. How he responds to these calls from day to day, from moment to moment, means success or failure for Christ and His Church. It determines his own spiritual growth or decay. In the little tests of daily life Christ's redemptive work triumphs or fails, the Body of Christ grows stronger or weakens, peace and love spread throughout the world or are limited, a lover of God or a lover of self is fashioned.

Few of us frequently have to face tough decisions, searing temptations, or overwhelming pressures. But each one of us daily faces the decision of opening heart and mind, or closing them off, to the people and responsibilities close at hand. How we respond at that moment matters immensely to ourselves, to Christ and His Church, and to all men. To keep my heart open right now to the Holy Spirit—that's the most important thing in the world for me at this moment.

For it is right now that I am asked to love, to forget myself, to serve. Not tomorrow, not next week or next month—but right now. Right now the Holy Spirit is ready to assist my weakness, to melt my heart of stone, to shake off my lethargy. Right now the powerful forces of faith and hope and love can be unleashed in me.

I *can* walk another mile with whoever forces me to go for one mile. I *can* refrain from judging. I *can* concentrate on the moment's duty. I *can* turn the other cheek. I *can* be patient in an unpleasant situation. I *can* trust in God. I *can* ask forgiveness for my sins. I *can* express my sorrow to a person whom I have offended.

But all this requires a certain self-control. If my first reaction to a person or a task is one of resentment or fear or rejection, I must see clearly that this is my moment of struggle, my opportunity, my challenge. This is the price all must pay for growth in maturity, in responsibility and in love. I must appreciate that my response matters to Christ and to all men. I must quickly cry to the Holy Spirit abiding within me, and thus will love grow among men and evil decrease.

Christ has told us that "the kingdom of heaven has suffered violence, and the violent take it by force" (Mt. 11:12). Who are the violent? Those who do violence to themselves, who struggle with their unhealthy emotions, who pray for a warm and merciful heart. Those who live dependently upon the Lord and who rely solely upon the power of His love. Those who desire to become passionate lovers of the God who is love.

Each time they allow Christ to triumph in them, all men feel the effects of His redemption, and the terrible ordeal of Calvary has been made once again worthwhile. And the parousia draws nearer, that is, Christ's kingdom of peace and of love.

As previous generations, we too carry the burden of many problems — with this immense difference, that the problems facing us are urgent and of mammoth proportions. Daily we read or hear of wars and danger of greater wars. We read of the poor and of immense injustice and greed. The experts propose plans to solve these problems. But all of their plans depend for success on one condition: that men love one another. In the measure in which men care for one another, cooperate with one another, sacrifice for one another, in that measure will we resolve the seemingly impossible difficulties of our age.

If we love one another! If there is love among men, then will the danger of nuclear warfare be averted. Then will the hungry be fed and the naked clothed and the ignorant instructed. Then, and only then. With this truth in mind, how can we refuse the little struggles of daily life? How can we not exercise our own God-given power to love so that the world may be healed?!

Wash Me
Still More
From My
Guilt

Love has many enemies.
Its power can be curtailed or destroyed by sin which
consists in refusing to love or be loved. Every sin
contains elements of pride, of self-assertiveness,
of self-sufficiency. Every sinner is a thief. We take
that which does not belong to us. We want to get for
ourselves what we want, when we want and as we
want. We play God for a moment. And love dies within us. All this is clear enough.

Other enemies of love are not so easily recognized. There are negative emotions, those more or
less vague and nagging resentments, fears, anxieties,
feelings of depression, of inadequacy, of guilt. They
can interfere with the full play of love. They can
limit it's scope and intensity. They can be destructive. Where love unites, these separate. Where love
builds, these tear down. Where love yields, these
refuse.

Consider those feelings of guilt, for instance,
which come over us in waves at times so powerful
that our solidly built house—at least we thought it
solid—shakes to its very foundations and threatens

106

to crumble completely. Guilt indeed is a powerful emotion too little recognized by us.

Without attempting to give an exact definition of guilt, let us indicate some of its more prominent elements: awareness of having done something bad, of desiring to do something bad, of being bad, coupled with the fear of condemnation by men and by God. A crippling thing, isn't it? How can one love God or neighbor if he constantly expects to be rejected? How can such a one believe that he is loved? How can he expect from life anything but dreariness? Let us look more closely at the phenomenon of guilt so as to become more free of its lethal effects on love.

Three kinds of guilt come to mind. First there is the guilt which I call *basic* or fundamental. It lies at the very heart of our nature. We are born members of a sinful race, as David wrote:
"Indeed, in guilt was I born,
    and in sin my mother conceived me" (Ps. 51:7).

We are members of a race somehow alienated from God. A corporate disobedience lives on in our moments of confusion, darkness, and rebellion. And this moral cancer chews at our insides. Our race's rejection of God, the Source and Origin of life, is the glaring untruth, and we give it new life each time we act as if we were self-sufficient, each time we forget that *without me you can do nothing.*

Basic guilt is cured by faith and humility. True, we are a sinful race, but we have been forgiven. Christ has saved us. At baptism we were washed clean of the race's sin. We experienced mercy. Let us believe in our baptism and we will rejoice. We will see and understand that now we are no longer slaves but beloved children, brothers of Christ, heirs of that kingdom which begins here on earth. When we are tempted to forget who we are, let us call on that liberating virtue, humility, to bring us back to reality.

Secondly there is *personal* guilt. We do something wrong deliberately and consciously. We know it is wrong. We do it because we want to do it. We do it freely. We have committed a real sin. We are truly guilty. What should a Christian do after such an act? Fret, stew, chew his finger nails, despair? He should be sorry, sorry that he has rejected the love of His Father. He should confess his fault and say, "I'm sorry." Then, he should rest happy in the knowledge that he has been forgiven, secure once again in God's love. And he should go on joyfully to perform some acts of penance.

It is good to carry our inward act of sorrow to some outward manifestation of fasting or alms-giving, as the Church has always advised. Let us pass up a meal once in a while and give the price of it to the poor. Devout Jews drink nothing but water for a whole month each year. Moslems during Ramadan neither eat nor drink before sundown each day. We can do as much for a day.

When we are truly guilty, let us be simple about it: admit it, confess it, ask forgiveness, believe that we are forgiven, and atone (which means become at-one again). We need the heart of a child always, even when we are forgiven, to really believe that our Father has forgotten the past forever.

Thirdly, there is *neurotic* guilt. Psychology here uses the term "feelings of guilt." One "feels" guilt who actually has no reason for such guilt. One "feels" deserving of severe punishment for little or perhaps no reason. One despairs of ever being accepted by God or man—and he cannot exactly say why.

These gray feelings, in moments of calm, remain somewhat inactive like a quiet volcano, yet their vague and distant rumblings produce a certain undefinable uneasiness. A mere word, a memory, a desire, almost anything can trigger a full explosion. A simple reprimand, a mistake, a small failure may cause severe distress to one who suffers from this neurosis. A heavy veil falls upon his mind. He becomes confused. He cannot concentrate on the work at hand. Depressive thoughts assail him such as "I am no good.... I have done evil.... I am evil.... there is no hope for me.... I can never be good."

Such a person is unable to think straight, to separate fact from fancy, to distinguish between true guilt and imaginary guilt. Self-punishment usually follows in the acceptable form of psychosomatic illnesses — headaches, nausea, colitis.

How is neurotic guilt cured? It all depends. One who is frequently overwhelmed by these painful feelings may do well to seek competent professional help. For others, a little heart-to-heart conversation with oneself may be all that is required. Am I really guilty of something? Did I actually *do* something wrong? The first step to freedom consists in separating fact from fancy. One may answer, "Yes, I did do something wrong, but I admitted it and was forgiven." Another: "Yes, I did something wrong. I will confess it to the Lord." Still another: "I did wrong but did not mean to do it; therefore I am not guilty." Or: "I really did nothing wrong, so there is nothing to feel guilty about." Or: "I'm just afraid that I will do something wrong. I must live more dependently upon God today so as to be strengthened by Him again tomorrow."

In such a sincere conversation with ourselves, the truth of the matter will often come to light. And after we have talked it over with ourselves, let us talk it over with God so that, during such trying moments, we may experience the full power of His love to heal us from every kind of guilt.

Only God Can Fulfill Us

God is love. He loves us so much that He reserves for Himself the very core of our personality, the essence of our being. Our attempts to communicate fully with another human being always end up in mystery, or in frustration. We want to share, to possess and be possessed, to understand and be understood, but we never quite make it. Man and wife, very much in love, still remain something of a mystery to each other, something of strangers.

Let us not be frustrated by this fact of our human experience. Let us rejoice. It means that no amount of human appreciation, understanding, or love can satisfy the human heart. We are made for God, for the Infinite, for a greater love affair than we can imagine. The core of our being, the mystery which each one of us is, our innermost self, is God's personal and exclusive domain. He alone knows our name. He alone knows us completely. He alone enters the enclosed garden. He alone—lover, gardener, redeemer—can heal our deepest wounds by His secret grace and make us truly come alive.

110

Daily we make the grave mistake of hoping we will be fulfilled. We think we can find perfect peace and joy if only certain changes are made or happen. We say to ourselves: "Everything would be okay if only my husband showed greater appreciation...if only I had a better job...if only...if only...." As long as we really believe that all will be well "if only" we haven't got the picture yet. As long as we strive to satisfy the immense longings of our hearts with anything less than God, our efforts are bound to be frustrating.

It is wise to specify clearly what we can expect from people and what we can expect only from God. It is wise to seek peace, joy, and fulfillment where they can be found. People can give us much, but they cannot give us everything. We need others, but they cannot fully satisfy us. They need us, but there are limits to what we can do for them.

We are made for a relationship of love with God, as well as with others. As a matter of fact, true love, true communication, cannot take place between two people unless each has filled his inner solitude with God—unless each seeks union with God as his basic purpose. Now to seek after God means to open one-self to God, to turn to Him in faith and trust, to be receptive to His activity and to respond to it. And all this will involve pain, darkness of understanding, misunderstanding, waiting, trusting, accepting. It will involve dying to self in many different ways.

God is love, and love means unselfishness. We are selfish. To be united to Him means to become un-selfish. If we truly seek after Him, He will see to it that we become unselfish. The tender knife of His love will cut us off from many satisfying opportunities and leave us gasping at times, hurt, weak, and alone.

But this is only so as to heal us, strengthen us, and fill us with Himself.

The demands of our surroundings, the duty of the moment, people, events and circumstances — God uses them all to purify us. Each day brings its opportunities, its challenges, its graces to the one who seeks after God. Each day we can respond, by His grace. Each day we can come out of our selfishness; we can love.

The Christian is engaged in a struggle. He has been chosen to bring others the good news of God's love, news about the Incarnation of His Son, His saving act, and His continued presence among us. But he needs mightily to develop the strong and joyful virtue of trust. Who can remain faithful to God without deep trust in His love and care? Who can walk through the dark passages of life without the guiding lamp of trust? Who can face an unselfish day without confidence in God's power?

God has made us for Himself. A joyful thought! But also a frightening thought! What does it mean? Will I have to give up everything? Shall I journey alone, with no consoling hand at my side? Will I find God, or will He forever elude me? In giving to others, how shall *I* be refreshed and restored? Is life with God a mere illusion born of dissatisfaction with human relationships?

Assuredly, with such doubts bombarding us, trust, hope, and confidence in God are needed. These attitudes will grow from trial to trial, from test to test. And through them all, God will reveal how trustworthy He is, that He does care, that He does love us with all the power of His infinite life.

In
Weakness,
Strength

Christ is alive. He lives in the Christian and the Christian is able to love, to serve, to forgive, to be compassionate because of the power of Christ's love in him — not because of his own power, but because his own natural power, talents, and life have been purified, transformed, suffused, and penetrated by the life of Christ, His power, His love; because these have been united with and completely subjected to them; because he is incorporated into Christ.

To a mature Christian, *to be* means to experience the power of the Christ who lives in us. And no one can experience the power of Christ except through the experience of his own weakness, the loss of his natural securities, the failure of his own attempts. St. Paul declared: "I wish to know Christ and the power flowing from his resurrection; likewise to know how to share in his sufferings by being formed into the pattern of his death. Thus do I hope that I may arrive at the resurrection from the dead" (Phil. 3:10-11).

St. Paul rejoices at his weakness, at his limitations, at his frustrations. He rejoices at the loss of all things. He wants to carry his share of human suffering, so as to *know* Christ, so as to experience the power of Christ in himself. "For when I am powerless, it is then that I am strong" (2 Cor. 12:10).

Man is a contingent being, that is to say, we can conceive of ourselves as not absolutely necessary and as having a very precarious hold on the existence we do possess. Man has not put himself together, nor does he hold himself together. Whether he is conscious of it or not, he is held together by God. Man, in his arrogance, forgets this only too easily. The arrogant man is precisely the one who exercises his own causality independent of God — or imagines he does. He tries to act in his own power, to control them for his own purposes.

And thus he lives a lie. He lives in illusion. He thinks he is a god, that he has made himself, that he acts by himself. He wants things his way, not the way they are. Lucifer stands as the supreme example of arrogance, of the son who rejects his father, of the creature who denies his Maker. "All these will I bestow on you," he says, "if you prostrate yourself in homage before me" (Mt. 4:9). He is the supreme schizophrenic, completely out of reality, living in a world of his own making.

I suffer from original sin. In me the tendency to arrogance, to unreality, to illusion, to self-assertion, to independence has deep roots. A part of me is made up of refusal, of denial, of rejection; a part of me does not want to bow its head, to enter the healing stream of reality, to receive love and life. My desire for self-assertion is my greatest weakness, my deepest sin. I need Christ, His healing power, His love.

I want to be strong. I want to control my environment. I want to be appreciated for myself. I'll try anything to hold myself together, to get what I want, to shore up the sagging walls of my house. And when I do that, I live a lie, I live in unreality, I am not myself, I am not real and authentic.

But the Lord, in His tender mercy, allows me to experience my limitations, to be frustrated in my most carefully laid plans, to fail. And that is the moment of grace. At that moment I can be real, I can be my true self, I have the opportunity of knowing who I really am...weak, poor, dependent, sinful. At that moment my free will faces a choice: rebel against reality, or receive healing and power and life from the risen Christ.

The sinner refuses. The saint accepts. The saint agrees to the saving action of Christ; he gives his weak power to the Lord to be changed, purified, and transformed. United with Christ, the saint's human qualities, far from being destroyed, are filled with a greater beauty, a greater strength. The saint never hopes to be strong with his own strength. The saint never hopes to "get over" his weakness. He never hopes to "make the grade." For he knows that he has made the grade each time he offers his weakness to Christ, each time he says, "The life I live now is not my own; Christ is living in me" (Gal. 2:20).

I am real, I am my true self, I am authentic when I experience my weakness, my limitations, my incapacity, my uselessness. I am great, I am strong, when I offer this true self to Christ, when I put my weight on Him. Then I live in the power of His love — the greatest and only security.

God Keeps
His
Promises

Fidelity is a beautiful characteristic, the fair flower of love. In God it shines in all its glory. He made us a promise, and He keeps His promise. I turn away from Him, but when I return He always receives me with joy. He's glad to have me back. And He never tires of forgiving, no matter how inconstant I may be, no matter how selfish and ungrateful. God is faithful, indeed He is! Praise be to Him, now and forever!

He allows me real freedom. And how often in my heart do I seek my joy away from Him! Francis Thompson writes:

> I tempted all His servitors, but to find
> My own betrayal in their constancy,
> In faith to Him their fickleness to me,
> Their traitorous trueness and their loyal deceit.

And when I finally come back, He is there waiting. He seems to find joy in me, in my presence, in my little love. He gives me lavishly new life, new strength, new understanding of His love. God is faithful, indeed He is. Praise be to Him, now and forever!

How can I be shocked at inconstancy among God's people now or in past history! I am the Church and people like me make it up. I cannot doubt for a moment the Lord's love for the Church when He has been so faithful and patient with me.

I used to think that the story of Hosea applied only to Israel. But today it seems clear that it applies to God's people at every stage of history.
"Again the Lord said to me:
Give your love to a woman
 beloved of a paramour, an adulteress;
Even as the Lord loves the people of Israel,
 though they turn to other gods" (Hos. 3:1).

"There is no fidelity, no mercy,
 no knowledge of God in the land" (Hos. 4:1).

True, we fluctuate so much in our loyalty to the Lord, to His Gospel, to His Spirit—how often we grieve that Spirit! We speak of faith, and forget that our commitment is to the holy and glorious Person of Jesus Christ. We get involved in all kinds of questions, attempts to change structures, social action projects — all of which are important and necessary—and yet, the name of the Lord is rarely spoken among us. We forget about our personal relationship with Him which should influence everything that we do.

In the midst of this inconstancy, the Lord does not reject us. His love remains constant and true. His Spirit, active and alive, calls us back to the source of our healing and our joy. His Spirit is ever active in our hearts, nudging us gently to remember that Jesus is a Person, our healing, our hope. The Spirit will whisper today those same words of consolation that He whispered to Hosea those many years ago:

"I will heal their defection,
  I will love them freely;
  for my wrath is turned away from them.
I will be like the dew for Israel:
  he shall blossom like the lily;
He shall strike root like the Lebanon cedar,
  and put forth his shoots.
His splendor shall be like the olive tree
  and his fragrance like the Lebanon cedar.
Again they shall dwell in his shade and raise grain;
They shall blossom like the vine,
  and his fame shall be like the wine of Lebanon....
Let him who is wise understand these things;
  let him who is prudent know them.
Straight are the paths of the Lord,
  in them the just walk,
    but sinners stumble in them" (Hos. 14:5-10).

Living Out Our Baptism

Jesus stands on the banks of the river Jordan, near Jericho, some twenty-five miles from Jerusalem. A crowd is there listening to John the Baptizer, a man of peace preaching repentance for sins. His words about the coming of a new kingdom reach the hearts of the people. Boldly they walk into the river to be washed clean of their sins, to be made ready for this kingdom.

Jesus stands there a long time, absorbing this moment, letting each second resound in His human heart. He too is a man, a man in love with the Father. He is God and man. He loves God and man. He unites God and man. He is the union of God and man. He steps into the river and His flesh blesses the waters forever, so that water ever afterwards may in turn hold a blessing for all men. He is a man who has been shaped and formed and made truly a man over a long training period by working with hammer and nails and wood. Son of God though He was, from the first He entered fully the human condition. Now He continues His entrance into that humanity as He walks into the waters, so great is His love for us, so great His love for the Father.

119

"Immediately on coming up out of the water he saw the sky rent in two and the Spirit descending on him like a dove. Then a voice came from the heavens, 'You are my beloved Son. On you my favor rests'" (Mk. 1:10-11). Father, Son, and Holy Spirit are briefly revealed, as is their oneness in love. Jesus is revealed as the Son, the new Israel, the new people of God. And He begins to make for God a new people. He prays, He teaches, He heals, He suffers.

The new people of God, initiated at Jesus' baptism, increase now from century to century. Through Baptism, men, one by one, are added to Jesus Christ. The Incarnation, the union of God with His people, grows and expands, straining mightily for that day when "there shall be one Christ loving Himself" (St. Augustine).

God so loves the world, all men without exception, that He sent His Son to bring them peace, love, happiness, healing, life in abundance. The Beloved of the Father is the servant of all men, His brothers. Isaiah says:

"Here is my servant whom I uphold,
    my chosen one with whom I am pleased,
Upon whom I have put my spirit;
    he shall bring forth justice to the nations....
A bruised reed he shall not break,
    and a smoldering wick he shall not quench,
Until he establishes justice on the earth;
    the coastlands will wait for his teaching" (Is. 42:1-4).

"I, the Lord, have called you for the victory of justice,
    I have grasped you by the hand;
I formed you, and set you
    as a covenant of the people
    a light for the nations,
To open the eyes of the blind,

to bring out prisoners from confinement,
and from the dungeon those who live in darkness"
(Is. 42:6-7).

These powerful words of Isaiah are spoken to us
today, for we are the Christ—His hands and His
heart. Would that we believed in the power of our
baptism, our anointing of the Spirit, as the Lord Jesus
Christ believed in His mission! What transformations
would occur around us! How many people would
find hope and peace and encouragement and life at
their meeting with us!

Jesus brings light to the blind. We too have that
tremendous power, since His truth lives on in us. Do
we believe that we can be a light to our neighbor's
feet? Jesus frees captives from prison. We too, through
love and concern, can bring a retarded child out of
his prison at least a little, or a fearful man out of his
fear, or a dejected woman out of her dejection. There
are prisons stronger than iron bars!

Most of all, may the Holy Spirit grant us a deep
faith, a passionate faith, in the value of prayer. Just
as we share in Christ's power to heal and to open
prisons, so too may we share in His power of prayer.
Let us ask and ask and ask, tirelessly, ceaselessly,
confidently. *Your Father hears your request.* Let us
believe in His love.

What Do You Mean I Can't Love!

We find it difficult to love. We want to give of ourselves. We want to appreciate others, to be considerate and thoughtful. And frequently, we find ourselves inconsiderate, thoughtless, unloving. The source of love has dried up inside of us. A sincere Christian, in these painful circumstances, should not despair but ask himself why.

Most often it is because we think that we can love by ourselves, that love originates from us. A serious error. We cannot love. It is absolutely impossible for us to make a single act of love, without the help of Christ. He said so: "Apart from me you can do *nothing*" (Jn. 15:5). He means it. We should believe Him. We should take Him literally. *We can do nothing.* Without Him we cannot make the least act of love.

True Christian love is a gift from God. He gives it at baptism, He increases it at confirmation, at every Mass and Holy Communion. Let us settle this question for ourselves once and for all. We have no love. We are selfish. Each forms in himself a little island of selfishness, with a hundred tentacles beating the air seeking satisfaction. God alone produces miracles. Christ alone changes the water of egotism into the strong wine of love. Let us be peaceful about that: we have no love; *caritas* is a gift from the God who is love.

To receive *caritas* from God with profit a person must be at peace. The seed of wheat cannot take root and grow in restless soil. The seed of grace, of love, cannot take root or grow in restless souls. That is why so many communions seem to have been received with so little profit. The fruits are weak. Millions of people flock to church on Sundays and line up for communion. They offer Christ to His Father; He offers Himself and them; He gives Himself and His infinite love to them. Yet little seems to happen. Materialism remains a strong philosophy; selfishness, a strong motivation. Christ's love does not seem to have penetrated very far into our secular institutions such as economics, education, recreation, and so on.

The seed has been sown. Christ's love is given in infinite abundance to us. Yet, it does not grow. We receive it and it disintegrates in our bosom. We take His gift and keep it for ourselves. And there it rots. Our selfishness scandalizes others.

A spiritual creature receives only to give. What it keeps for itself will become a problem. A spiritual creature receives for itself by giving the gift it has received. Love is given to us abundantly, but because we try to squander it on ourselves and not pass it on to others, it vanishes like smoke on a windy day.

And we do not pass it on, I suggest, because we do not receive it in a soul at peace. Peace is the tranquillity of order. When we have set our house in order, peace will come. The soul will then be disposed to receive Christ's love. It will grow. It will produce much fruit.

Two statements found in the Scriptures produce great peace, but only in the measure in which we live them, in the measure in which we make them our own. The first was mentioned above, "Apart from me you can do nothing" (Jn. 15:5). When we find ourselves restless and unpeaceful, anxious, dissatisfied, concerned, let us ask why. We will find that self, in some way or another, is again putting its worst foot forward. Pride, me, my own way, are the causes of unpeace. We've been trying "to do it by ourselves." We've been trying to assert ourselves. We have forgotten that without Christ we can do nothing.

This is a difficult lesson to learn. Most of us need "to reach the end of our rope," "to fall flat on our faces," before we even begin to appreciate this simple and obvious truth. When we have floundered around for a while in the confusing whirlpool of our own ideas, when living and loving have become totally impossible, when all consolation and all joy have shrivelled up within us, then perhaps we turn to God. Then perhaps we appreciate a little that without Christ and His constant sustaining love, virtue and joy will escape us forever.

Self-knowledge is the foundation of the spiritual life, says St. Catherine of Siena. That kind of self knowledge which helps us to see that of ourselves we can do nothing—that is what she is talking about. When all our security has disappeared, when all our props have been taken away, when we see our utter weakness and sinfulness—that is to approach the foundation. Such a revelation is a great grace. If the soul gradually turns to God, she will realize that

He is the source of all her life, of all her love, of all her strength. With growing amazement she will experience, and deeply experience, the second half of reality: "In him who is the source of my strength I have strength for everything" (Phil. 4:13). She will love with Christ's love. Christ will love in her. The power of her love will be diffused to the ends of the earth.

So when we find ourselves unloving, let us examine what makes us unpeaceful. It is self. Let us turn to God and ask Him to fill us with the power of His love for today. He certainly will.

Portrait
of a
Would-be
Apostle

Let us look at a certain type of Christian who presents himself to the Church with a desire to "change society for the better." Unless we see this man as he is, as a product of the very society which he is called upon to transform, we will not have an adequate picture of the task to be done. With a few modifications, similar things could be said about women as well.

First, his religious equipment. He may know little about God, about Christ, about the life-giving sacraments, about the Eucharist, about the Gospel. To him God is mostly Someone to be feared, and not to be loved. He does not really believe that God is love. He has learned to abide by certain rules of moral conduct. He avoids certain sins. He says a number of prayers. But there is no evidence of life in him. He does not nourish that life. He does not practice virtue.

Mesmerized by a limited number of sins such as sexual abuses, intoxication and swearing, the commandment of love, whether of God or of neighbor, leaves him cold. He is satisfied with not doing what he considers deliberate and conscious harm to his neighbor. He does not love his neighbor. He has adjusted to certain superficial relationships with others which are socially acceptable and superficially satisfying.

Spiritually, therefore, we have here an empty man, who knows not his God, or knows Him wrongly. A man half dead, in whom the flame of grace barely flickers. A man who does not even realize that the spiritual life is a *life*. And so he comes to be trained to change the world. In his mind, this means learning superficial principles and techniques whereby he can help in "making the world a better place to live in." He wants to discover simple means which will produce big results. He thinks that with a little bit of training he will be able to change the world. This is equivalent to fighting atomic weapons with a trusty pea-shooter.

Emotionally he is unstable, fearful, rigid. Changes upset him and average pressures overwhelm him. He becomes easily discouraged and frustrated. Communication with others in depth frightens him.

Physically, he has neglected his body; he is flabby. He despises manual labor. He has little or no manual dexterity. His father never taught him crafts, skills, and often not even hobbies.

Intellectually, his appraisal of men and events conforms to newspapers and to public opinion. His education has taught him to talk, not to think. He knows little of philosophy, literature, and the arts. His conversation remains trite. He sees problems at a surface level. He proposes solutions equally ephemeral and ineffectual. In this person the problems of society stand clearly revealed. We see in depth the work to be done.

Now this man is certainly of good will. The Holy Spirit is moving him. His desire to do something for God and man is valid and beautiful to behold. But he needs training — spiritually, emotionally, physically, intellectually. He needs to be transformed. He needs to discover life. Christ will resurrect him. This candidate will undergo much pain, many doubts, much darkness as he begins to see himself as he is, in his misery, his emptiness, his ignorance. Slowly he will begin to live. The spiritual life will become a *life* in this renewed human nature. He will resurrect and then go on to be an instrument of resurrection for others.

We face a de-humanized and de-Christianized world. It cannot be humanized and Christianized by mediocre methods and mediocre people. We are called by Christ to do an almost impossible work. Few men and women have understood and evaluated both the problem and the solution. People need to be prepared in depth. Who will provide that preparation? Who wants to undergo such a training course? Only fools, fools for Christ, who want to die to an artificial self and live in the power of Christ's love so that many may truly live also.

May You Live All the Days of Your Life!

The ability to enjoy life and to love are closely connected. For our God is both the God of love and of the living. He has made us to live, both here on earth and in heaven, before and after death, now and forever. By enjoyment of life I do not mean "having a good time." I do not mean a constant round of parties and entertainment. I mean the ability to respond to beauty, to goodness, to pain. The capacity for wonder and amazement and delight. The openness to be healed of life's daily wounds by the sight of a single flower, a kind word, or a joke.

Things are amazing, people are delightful. God made them all. He made them and rejoiced, for He saw that they were good. That is the truth of the matter. We too can rejoice for they are there, right in front of us, soliciting our response.

God is our Father. Through His Word, His Son, He made all things, and He continues His work of creation. Towards the end of one of the solemn prayers (Canon) of the Church, we are told that it is through Him, Christ, that God unceasingly creates all these good things, makes them holy, gives them life, blesses them, and bestows them on us. All things and every person come from the loving hand of inexhaustible Creativity. Every thing, every person, reveals the Master's touch. Every person is rich with perfection, resplendent with beauty and immensely attractive.

Every person, therefore, is precious, good, lovable, enjoyable. God, who loves us so much, wills that every thing and especially every person should bring us joy, should liberate the life that is in us, should lead us out of the desert of self. Life is in us — a huge reservoir of strength and joy, given by our Father, a real share of His own infinite joy and strength and love. The Christian does not only seek after moral justice. The Christian does not only try to "do the proper thing." He has been directed to love. He has been set on the path of love by his Baptism. He has been consecrated to love.

He has been consecrated, therefore, to life. He opens his eyes, his heart, his mind to reality, responding to all that is, simply because it is, and thereby he lives. He becomes a loving, living person. He responds to all that God has made, natural and supernatural. He responds to the things and the people around him. He responds to the Word of God and to the sacraments. Thus he becomes a person in whom nature and supernature are so enmeshed as to be indistinguishable. He becomes the person God intended him to be.

A lady said of St. Francis de Sales: "He shows me so much respect and reverence, but I do not know if it is because he is a gentleman or because he is a saint."

Our enemy, the devil, brings us boredom, discouragement, despair. He is the thief who comes only to steal, and slay, and destroy. He tries hard to rob us of love, of joy, of hope, of life. But Christ is with us. He has conquered boredom, discouragement, and despair.

"I came
that they might have life,
and have it to the full" (Jn. 10:10).

Christ unites all men and all things. He is the center of the universe. In His presence, God embraces all men and all material things. Not only does Christ stand in the middle, He is the middle. From Him all life comes to us, all hope, all joy, all love.

And how does He bring us life and hope and joy and love? By His word — the Sacred Scriptures — a living, healing, consoling word, a strengthening word. By His sacraments, most of all the Eucharist. We partake of Him who is life and love. We are filled each time, with life and love.

Jesus brings us life by every thing that exists. A single blade of grass contains within itself the science of botany and the secret of life. Truly it proclaims the glory and the love of God. He brings us life by every act of love manifested to us by another person. "Love one another as I have loved you" (Jn. 15:12). He gave us that power, that tremendous power.

By love we can free one another, we can help another free himself, we can liberate in him the life which is there. We can do that for one another by genuine love.

How great is our need for each other's love, understanding, and patience! Each time we refuse to love another person, that person lives a little less, dies a little. Each time we give love, we die a little to selfishness but rise to a greater life, and the other lives a little more of true life. If we love one another, we shall live and live and live. If we don't, we shall die little by little to the only true life there is — love.

Let no one dare say: "I am not needed. I am unimportant." That is a denial of Christ's work and plan. No one can dare to be indifferent to another person, or fail to have mercy. "Love one another" (Jn. 15:12), He said. He knows the power of His love in us. He loved completely, "to the end" (Jn. 13:1) and we were reconciled with our loving Father. He wants us to love each other so that we may believe in this reconciliation and enjoy its fruits.

It is a fantastic thought that at each moment I can, in a way, bring life or death to another person. I can accept or condemn. I can love or destroy. Where love is, life is, and beauty and joy. Burdens become light, and we more readily perceive the goodness of people and things.

And when we feel that a person does not love us, let us be patient, for love, according to St. Paul, is first of all patient. It waits. It trusts. It does not pressure people. It is humble. God has to purify us. "If you love those who love you," says the Lord, "what merit is there in that? Do not tax collectors do as much?" (Mt. 5:46) Only a broken heart can be transformed into a heart of flesh, into a merciful heart, a loving heart. Without experiencing pain, no one can become a lover, no matter how much he has been loved. Christ taught that by His words and His actions. We need to love in order to live, but we must struggle mightily not to be crushed when love is refused. Blessed are those who live and who love daily.

Relax
Once
in a
While

To relax or not to relax, that is the question. Our immediate answer would be to want to relax all the time, but we know that both leisure and activity are necessary if one wants to be a mature person and a mature Christian. In our own day, many people seem to have forgotten how to relax, though.

God knows how much our generation needs to relax, to simmer down, to be quiet inside and outside, to develop our capacities of contemplation and wonder. Husbands who are caught in the economic rat-race need wives who know how to be at peace. Husbands need to be refreshed and restored at the end of a feverish day by a woman who has prayed and who has been in tune with the deeper and silent sources of creative life. Such men will return to the marketplace on the morrow with a renewed vigor and a clearer vision of reality.

Dr. V. Voyer, a renowned psychiatrist, put it this way: "What the world needs is less committees and more meditation." Not that Dr. Voyer wants to abolish all committees—he's on quite a few himself. But he knows the sterility of mere activism. Our generation desperately needs to relax. Alcohol, tranquilizers, T.V., travel—all these may give temporary relief from anxiety, but they cannot cure our restlessness. Only love can and does.

Awareness of love brings peace, healing, tranquility, joy. Awareness of being loved brings about relaxation. Deep awareness of being loved by God brings peace, stability and strength, the strength to face the many tensions which are part and parcel of life.

The relaxed and peaceful Christian knows that, in one sense, he cannot relax, that he never has everything "figured out," that there are no sure and secure blueprints for him to follow, that he must constantly be open to the inspirations of the Holy Spirit. Chosen by the Lord, he is engaged in a warfare, a struggle, that ends only at death.

Each day presents challenges to his faith, his trust, his love. Love never sleeps, never quite relaxes. Love remains always on the alert. Even in its most tired moments, love hears the cries of hungry and lonely men and women, the wail of suffering children, the pain of Christ. Love hears and prays and agonizes with every agony. Love thinks and plans and serves. Love rushes to heal, to console, to enfold.

Daily the "relaxed" Christian is faced with tension-creating questions. How can I find time for prayer and yet prepare good meals for my family? What can I do for the hungry people of the world? Should I buy that new car or keep the old one and give some of the money to the poor? Do I buy or "make do"?

There are no stereotyped answers to the many practical problems facing one who tries to live the Christ-life. Change, development, renewal characterize our condition. We cannot be rigid, unchanging, inflexible.

To relax or not to relax. Both—and at the same time. Let us relax in the Lord's immense love and care, but not relax from the struggle, not be indifferent to pain, not escape from the day's challenges. More of us certainly need to learn how to relax in God's love and be strengthened by the power of His love in order to better meet the struggles of the day.

More Blessed To Receive Than To Give

To give, to receive. When and how to give, when and how to receive? What takes precedence in our minds, the gifts we receive or the gifts we give? Do we prefer to state our opinions and ideas or to listen to others? Would we rather give orders or receive orders? Do we let God take the initiative or do we? These are important questions. The answers we give determine much of our relationship with God and others.

I suggest that most of us prefer to give than to receive. It makes us feel important. This desire for self-assertion impedes communication among human beings and vitiates our relationship with God. It leads to frustration both in our human and divine contacts.

Three people sit around a table discussing world affairs. Now it is well known that in North America we are all experts on world affairs. Three persons, each with his own opinion, each wanting his opinion to be noticed and accepted, each quite sure of himself. Result: frustration, lack of communication, loneliness, because each wants to give and does not want to receive. We prefer to teach; to be taught is painful. It puts us in an inferior position. It forces us to acknowledge our ignorance. We forget that the admission of ignorance is the beginning of wisdom. It isn't who talks that matters; it's who has something to say.

A husband returns home after the proverbial hard day at the office. He wants to tell his wife all that he has done for her and the family. He wants his gift appreciated. She wants to tell him all that she has done for him and the family that day too. She wants him to appreciate her gift. This kind of thing can make people climb walls. Why? The answer is obvious, isn't it? Neither wants to receive the other's gift. And so they settle down to a moody martini and buzzing thoughts of self-pity: "I'm not appreciated. He (she) doesn't want to hear what *I* do every day. What am I doing here? If it weren't for the children, etc...?"

The self-sacrificing partner or parent is not always a loving partner or parent. The seemingly unselfish act can hide a lot of selfishness. When we give, it's awfully important to appreciate how much we have received, how much we are receiving.

In our relationship with God, we are completely on the receiving end. He has given us all that we are, all that we possess. He gives us our supernatural life. He sustains it through His word and the sacraments. He gives us Himself. He takes the initiative. We make a response. We agree to follow where He leads, to be transformed by His action. We cooperate. For we are creatures. We have nothing of our own, except our selfishness. We have no love except the love He places in us through His grace. We are an emptiness that must open itself to the great Giver to be filled.

To love means first of all to be loved. That is *our* situation. In the measure in which we receive God's love and the love of others, in that measure are we able to love God and others. True, the Scripture says that "there is more happiness in giving than receiving"(Acts 20:35). It is better because it is more God-like. But for us creatures, it is imperative that we first learn how to rejoice in receiving so as to be able to give. It has been succinctly put by Thomas Merton:

"Before you give yourself to others, you must have a self to give."

We become by receiving. We live and love and give by the power of God's love.

Oh, Heavenly Days!

What comes to your mind when you think of heaven? What kind of image do you have of life in eternity? What goes on in heaven? What types have "made it"? Those saints and angels, will they be interesting, pleasant, fun to associate with? Our Lady, St. Joseph, St. Michael, will they have any use for the likes of me? Will it be fun to talk with St. Thomas Aquinas, or will I feel like an ignorant crumb?

And the clear vision of God, what will that be like? *To know as I am known.* Will that be delightful or frightening? Will I be able to look upon the face of the living God without dissolving into the dust from whence I came?

Heaven is full of delights, of wonders ever renewed, of magnificent discovery followed by more magnificent discoveries. St. Paul told us that eye has not seen, ear has not heard, nor has it even occurred to man what God has prepared for those who love Him (cf. 1 Cor. 2:9). Isaiah, centuries before, had spoken in like manner concerning life with God begun here on earth and perfected in heaven.

What heaven will be like exactly we do not know. But some things we do know. It will be a place where love reigns supreme, where we shall be loved and shall love perfectly, where we shall be delighted by the sight of God and of all His people, and where we will delight others. It will be a place of ecstasy. We shall be drawn out of ourselves, and that must be one of the greatest joys of all! We shall be in ecstasy over the beauty, goodness, lovableness of God, of each person there, of the person next to you and me. And we'll have the same effect on others. We will know the thrill of falling in love with God, with our Lady, St. Joseph, and the least "prominent" person there.

How do I know that St. Thomas, St. Anthony, St. Ignatius Loyola, the Little Flower, St. Michael — all these tremendous people — will be my friends? Because nobody can enter heaven who is not a lover. That's what each person has become. He or she has obeyed Christ's command to love God and neighbor. He or she has died to selfishness. They now see with pure eyes the immense lovableness of each person, so they can love me. As a matter of fact, not only can they love me (if I'm there, that is, and I sure hope to be), but they can't *help* loving me. Love is now at work completely in all of them. Each one of them is a throbbing heart radiating something of the God of love Himself.

But we don't have to wait. Today, right now, the angels and saints are our lovers. They've "made it," and they long to see us "make it" too. So even now they love me. Even now we can communicate, we can get to know each other, we can be delighted by each other. Even now the grace that is in me, by the mercy of God, attracts them and delights them. It is such a beautiful thing they see in the soul of each Christian who is living in the love of Christ, that they are eager for its growth, its full flowering — for the sight of its full beauty.

No, the saints are not frightening, or boring, or censorious, or self-righteous. They are lovers. They love me even as I am — weak, inclined to sin, struggling with my selfishness. They enjoy my company. They like to talk with me. As a matter of fact, they even like me! And not just me, but you and you and you—all of us as we struggle with the selfishness in and around us, as we turn to the Lord for healing and strength. Now isn't that a very pleasant thought, a very pleasant fact?

Heaven is a place where nothing exists but love. Heaven is a continual state of love. Heaven opens its doors to lovers only, people who have struggled to die to selfishness and who have, by the mercy of God, acquired the capacity of being thrilled by the goodness and beauty of persons outside themselves. Everyone in heaven has been fashioned by God whose name is merciful love.

Yes, it will be joyous, ecstatically joyous. We will be filled with excitement by everything and everyone we see. We will appreciate that all this joy has come from the cross of Christ, and we will sing uninhibitedly (even those of us who belong to the Western tradition!) unrestrained praise to the Lord, with everything that we have and are.

Heaven can begin now; in fact it ought to. There we shall see the goodness, beauty, lovableness of God, our Lady, the angels and saints, of the persons next to us. Why not try and see now, with the eyes of faith, the same realities in the people with whom we live? Let's "practice" now. Otherwise we may not be able to play the game when we arrive!

Why not believe now in the immense love of God which shall delight us for all eternity? He is the same today whom we shall meet, the infinitely loving One by whose mercy we too can become lovers. He desires nothing more than that we begin to live right now, upheld by His transforming power of love, the life He has waiting for us for all eternity.

The Greatness
of the
Human Heart

Nothing in the whole world is as exciting, as beautiful, as rich as the human heart. Nothing is more important to the Church and to suffering mankind as the coming of the Lord into one of these hearts. By heart I mean the spirit in us, the core of our being, our true self, the person God has made and which He heals, transforms, uncovers. I mean the home of the Holy Spirit, the powerful and lavish God who loves each man and longs to enrich him. Such a heart—touched by God, opened by Him, alive with His love—is easily the most beautiful thing in the world, and the most healing thing *for* the world.

The great Teresa of Avila—Teresa of Jesus as she called herself—discovered the magnificence of her own heart. She wrote about it for our instruction and enrichment. She sees her heart as many beautiful castles, each containing any number of glorious rooms furnished and lavishly decorated by the Holy Spirit.

I like to think of the human heart as a vast land extending beyond the horizon into a growing light,

a land where wild and dangerous beasts are tamed
and come to live side by side in peace and harmony.
A land where thistles grow into soft, thick grass,
where sickly trees develop into majestic, shady
giants. A land where vultures turn into bright, ex-
otic birds, each singing its own pure song to the
Lord. For such is the desire and the power of the
Lord: to fashion a heart into the land of tomorrow,
the land of the peaceful kingdom of the Lord Jesus
Christ.

The human heart opened by the Spirit is a vast
house in which each man can find a room, *his* room,
specially made ready for him, a room that has been
waiting and longing for his coming, where he can
be healed, cleansed, clothed in new garments. The
human heart is a house where hundreds and thousands meet, really meet, and recognize each other at
long last, and know each other as brother and sister.

Who shall heal the deep wounds of the Church
and of the human spirit? We can, with the Lord's
help. He has given us this glorious power. We heal
others by receiving their pain into our hearts, by
allowing the Spirit to shape our hearts into tender
hospitals, by letting Him heal us of our sin. As I
am healed of my arrogance and fears, every man is
healed. For we stand as one before the Lord.

To contemplatives, to those who spend a great
deal of their time in prayer, and who at the present
time may be questioning the value of their vocation,
I am happy to be able to say: "I belong to a most
active, apostolic family. My family and I *know* from
brutal experience that mere activity leads only
to greater confusion and misery. Apostolic works
turn sour unless they flow from a transformed heart.
You are, oh, so needed by the suffering peoples of the

world. Your hearts are needed, your quiet life open
to God, your prayer, your love.

"You and people like you are the hope of all men.
Write much more than you do. Tell us of the wonderful works of God taking place in your own hearts
so that we too may come to know Him as you do.
Our hearts hunger for Him and we despair of ever
finding Him. Tell us that it happens, that He is
alive, that He lives in you. For many today it is hard
to believe that He is, let alone that He cares."

Our heart is so small when we first pay attention to it, when we discover it is there. And it hurts
to let another person in, another person's pain
and another person's beauty. It hurts because it
is so small. To grow big it must be stretched. Accept the suffering. Let the person in. The heart
is a tender, throbbing, finely meshed sieve enfolded
in the heart of Christ who lives in us. Let the person through to Christ who alone heals and restores.
And in some very mysterious way, the other person
returns from Christ to you, to heal your enlarged
heart, to give it a peace it never knew before.

Such is the greatness of our God. And you will
know that "it is in giving that you receive," that
life rises from death, that love heals both lover and
beloved. And you will praise God for His tender
mercy. Should your heart be closed and small and
fearful, be patient and wait upon the Lord, upon
your Day of the Lord. As a man put it the other day, a
man who has walked "through fire and water and darkness" into the land of the living: "For a long, long
time we must simply believe that one day God will
open our hearts Himself."

The world hungers for men who know God,
not just *about* God. It hungers for men who live
a new life, for their salt and their light. Christians

yearn for shepherds who will lead them to green pastures, who will free them from their fears and terrors, and prepare them for the coming of the Lord into their own hearts.

In these days full of noise and sickness, of confusion and unpeace, let Christians stand still inside, even when busy about many things. Let them be as people waiting for the return of the Master. *Be still, and know that I am God.* What a service this is to mankind. How beautiful, how healing, how powerful is the human heart waiting upon the Lord!

God
Is My
Friend

God is the Friend of man. God loves man. Already in the Old Testament He revealed Himself as a God who loves. Although Israel, His chosen people, His beloved, His bride, commits every sin of dark disloyalty, turns to pitiful gods, seeks happiness with dismal lovers, God never rejects her. He never abandons her. He keeps calling her back to Himself. He keeps forgiving her infidelities and drowning them in the ocean of His mercy.

God is the Friend of man. God loves man. The Word becomes man. He expresses His love not only in words but by stupendous actions. In His thrice-holy Person, the divine and the human are wedded for eternity in a union so strong that even death does not break in and destroy it. He rushes from the heart of Triune love, He leaps down into a mere woman's womb, the better to love us, to make us understand the immensity of God's love.

His actions, every one of them, and His words, every one of them, throb with love. Love desires to become one with the beloved. In Jesus Christ, our blessed Lord, God becomes one with man. Love chooses the lot of the beloved, lives his life, shares his joys and his pains. Jesus Christ adopts all the ways of men, sin excepted. He subjects Himself to all the laws which govern our lives. He experiences all the needs of the flesh, all our limitations, all our weakness, all our suffering.

Every one of us can say and must say, for it is the truth: "Jesus loves me so much that He chose to experience my way of life, my work, my difficulties, my weakness, my loneliness. He understands, for He has been through all this — and more — for me and because of me. He knew what burdens I was to carry, and He did not want me to carry them without Him. He has traveled every road I must travel. Deliberately, willingly, joyfully, He has preceded me wherever I may go and waits for me there. Simply because He loves me. Simply because He is love. Simply because He is the true God."

Sometimes we complain and say: "Why does God treat me this way? Why does He allow me to suffer? What have I done to Him that pain should enter my life?" Instead we should say: "Jesus knew that I would endure this pain, this difficulty, and that I would find it hard to bear. That is why He chose pain, to help me bear mine. How good God is! How much He loves me, a sinner, unworthy of any love!"

All men must work. Most men and women must work with their hands and earn their bread by the sweat of their brows. Most men labor at monotonous jobs — lifting, digging, hauling, making things on machines. Women the world over cook, clean, sew, wash, type, do office work. God loves us all. He deliberately chose to work at monotonous jobs. He worked mostly with His hands. He experienced aching muscles. He earned His bread as most men do. He deliberately chose for His mother and His foster-father simple, ordinary folk who lived simple, ordinary lives.

Every workingman, every farmer, every clerk, every truck-driver must say, for it is the truth: "The Son of God worked as I must work, with hands, muscles, and sweating brow, because He wanted to be as I am, because He passionately desired to share completely my way of life, because He loves me." And every housewife must say, for it is the truth: "The Son of God invited Mary, His Mother, to do the things that I do, for my comfort, my encouragement, and my joy."

The world despises manual labor. The Christian appreciates its value because of Christ, and because of those millions who labor with their hands. The world enslaves material things to its own selfish ends. The Christian treats them with respect, as fascinating gifts of a loving Father. The world worships technology. The Christian consecrates technological science to the service of God, by directing it to the service of mankind.

Service, identification, empathy—these are precious words in the glorious vocabulary of love! By His very life, Christ our Lord tells us how to live, how to love. "Love one another as I have loved you," (Jn. 15:12) He said at the Last Supper. *As I have loved you*—that's the key. He became one of us, one with us in nature and heart and mind that we might become one in mind and heart with other human beings.

He died to Himself daily that we might die to self today. He died on the cross to save us from our selfishness and show us the way to resurrection, to unselfishness, to love. He served us and goes on taking care of all our needs, that we might appreciate the immense value of serving one another. How much God loves us! And what a joy that we can love Him back right now by serving, understanding, loving each other in all the little things we are called to do!

Truly God is the Friend of man. Who can deny it? Let the Holy Spirit, the Spirit of love and of truth, the Spirit of Christ, teach you the one truth that really matters and which contains all the rest: that God is love, and that He loves *you* passionately. May He be free to act in you. May you die and resurrect through the thrilling power of His ineffable love!

From
Illusion
to
Diffusion

It seems to me that the Christian passes through four principal stages on his way to the God of love. The characteristics are, in progressive order: illusion, confusion, fusion, and diffusion. They are not clearly separated, but one or the other predominates according to the person's progress.

The initial stage is characterized by *illusion*. Not that the beginner lives in total illusion. Some truths he does apprehend. He is united (or fused) with Christ, to some extent. His love diffuses itself somewhat. But basically he suffers from illusions. He thinks he knows. He has everything pretty well figured out. He has confidence in himself, in his own ability. If his apostolic action seems weak and ineffective, he attributes it to factors outside of himself. Others are impeding his good work. He is not understood. He is not appreciated. He is not let free to do things which would be for the benefit of others. He believes primarily in action, in teaching, in organization. These are *the* means for the salvation of the world. He may speak of the cross as redemptive. But he doesn't act as though it is. For as soon as the cross casts its shadow over his life, he retires in panic to lick his wounds and indulge in criticism of others, in self-pity.

He may pray for trust, but he doesn't trust the value of trust. He trusts only when everything is cut and dry, when everything is clear, when everything makes sense. Therefore, he doesn't really trust. He may appreciate a little the value of love, but he quickly withdraws from love when its pain is revealed.

He does not truly love, although he thinks he does. He strives to be humble but he recoils from humiliations. He reads the words of Christ: *Without me you can do nothing.* He really tries to believe these words. But he doesn't. He is too well aware of the many things which his training, his knowledge, his ability can do. He rarely asks himself: "What does Jesus want of me today?" He is too busy determining the blueprint of his own life and activity... too engrossed with "what can Christ do for me today?"

Generous he is. He wants to give his love to God and to his neighbor. He wants to become a saint. He wants to dedicate himself, according to his vocation, to the growth of Christ's Body. But he wants to do everything according to his own ideas, according to his own plans. He wants to do God's will his way, not God's way. He wants to love, not to be loved. He wants to give, not to receive. He wants to be a creator, not a creature. And this is his illusion.

Gradually, by the grace of God, his efforts will fail. His plans will be wrecked. All his props will be taken away from him one by one, by the pitiless hand of a tender God. The jealous God who wants to be sole Master, Creator, and Lover cannot allow His creature to be under such illusions. And now *confusion* rages in his heart. Temptations which had not been experienced for years—disobedience, lust, laziness—mercilessly tear at his being. Darkness comes to live with him as in her own house. Frustration burns away at every fiber of his being. Virtue seems totally impossible. And love, beautiful love, reveals itself a bitter fruit.

Happy the man in such a state! He is being purified for intimate, healing union with God. Let him quiver but not waver. Let him be still under the searing pain. Soon he will enter the next glorious stage.

He is now ready for *fusion*. Fusion with God! Like the wood which must first be charred before it glows, he now begins to shine with God. His faith has become a living thing. He no longer believes in himself. He believes in God. He no longer trusts himself. He trusts in God. His love is God's love, *caritas*. And his activity takes on a depth and a power which years ago were totally unsuspected.

There is no fusion without immediate *diffusion*. If he remains intensely loyal to God's love, if he scorns self-love and pride when they manifest themselves, if he abides in God's love alone and never walks out of its stream, further illusions and confusions will not overwhelm him. His love will grow like a fire in the forest, a fire whipped by strong winds. It will diffuse itself and warm many hearts. It will repel evil as nothing else can. It will give untold glory to God who has become its sole Master.

The power of Christ's love will walk the earth in him.

Golden Memories of My Priesthood

La Fond, Alberta, around 1923

Archbishop Henry Joseph O'Leary, Archbishop of Edmonton, Alberta, is sitting in the rectory's big chair. He has sat me on his knee. He asks, "Do you want to be a priest? "I answer, "Yes, I do. I want to be a Jesuit." He asks, surprised, "Why?" I answer fearlessly, "Because they are priests of Jesus." A pained look comes over his face and he says, "And who do you think we are?"

St. Edmund's Parish, Calder, (Edmonton, Alberta)

A young man faints in school. The reason – malnourishment. The family has had only some potatoes to eat for the last two weeks. I ponder this event and realize that on the one hand, wheat is being left to rot in the fields, while on the other hand, people are going hungry! This strikes me as an anomaly. I ask myself, "Who shall correct this wrong?" The answer: "Lay people." "Who shall tell the lay people about this injustice? Who shall inspire them to do something about it?" The answer: "Priests." At that moment is born my vocation to the lay apostolate – to be a priest of the lay apostolate.

154

Edmonton, Alberta, Jesuit College, 1934

During a decision retreat, my excellent spiritual director, Father Alphonse-Marie Pelchat, S.J., tells me that I have no vocation to the Jesuit Order, but rather to the Diocesan priesthood.

The summer of 1936 - my last summer "in the world"

I live it up in Montreal and other places of Quebec partying nearly every night until the wee hours since I am convinced that entering the seminary is nearly equal to entering the cemetery. In my mind, life in a rectory is dull, boring, spent mostly in edifying conversations with pious people.

St. Joseph's Seminary, Edmonton, Alberta, 1936 - 1940

It's not really too bad. There are some fine, interesting professors – particularly Fr. Michael O'Neill, Father Paul Joseph O'Reilly, and the opportunity for invaluable friendships with seminarians from all over Western Canada – including the Ukrainian Diocese – and also, a lot of opportunity for research, for study of my favourite subject – history. Why history? Looking at the world around, I've been asking myself, "How did we get that way?" History provides a lot of answers.

St. Joseph's Cathedral, Edmonton, Alberta, June 23, 1940, 9:25 a.m.

Archbishop John Hugh McDonald has just imposed hands upon me, and anointed my hands of clay. The Master of Ceremonies, Fr. James Holland, leads me to the sacristy and there says, "Wash your hands **Father**." The immense weight I've carried all along – mainly the fear of a dull, boring life as a priest – lifts completely, never to return again. A new life, a new enthusiasm, a new power takes hold of me.

Legal, Alberta, June 24, 1940

At the banquet following my first Mass, the toastmaster invites me to speak. Archbishop McDonald whispers in my ear, "Now you may speak with authority!" I haven't stopped talking since.

Harlem, New York, August, 1940

Catherine de Hueck kneels at the corner of Lennox Avenue and 138th St. at 10 p.m. and says, "Give me your blessing, Father." Her faith in the priesthood reinforces my own faith mightily and sustains me all through my priestly life.

Clyde, Alberta, September, 1940

I sit in the confessional for the first time in my life. A centenarian is my first penitent. He says, "Bless me Father." He is 77 years my senior.

Morinville, Alberta, November, 1940

We've managed to organize seventeen study clubs on adult education, cooperatives, credit unions, and a couple on topics of special interest to youth. This makes me realize how good people are, how willing to help each other. Several people open their hearts to me. I begin spiritual direction. My first directee is a very holy young nun. (Still alive, still my directee, still very holy in 1990). A local farmer teaches me True Devotion to Our Lady, according to the Doctrine of St. Louis DeMontfort. In the rectory, to my great surprise, I discover that life can be not only bearable, but considerably interesting and happy. My pastor, Monsignor Maxime Pilon, gives me a lot of wise counsel. My first baptisms are the children of the local bootlegger. My first marriage – people who have been shacked up and living hidden in the bush. My first

Extreme Unction, as we used to say – an attempted
suicide, a lady in her forties. (She lived to a ripe old
age.)

April 11, 1941 – Fiftieth Anniversary of
St. John the Baptist Parish, Morinville

We honour the pioneers. One tells me, "The only
reason we stayed is because we couldn't get away!"

I see the hunger for God. At a study-club, I talk
about the doctrine of the Mystical Body of Christ –
hesitatingly, tentatively, shyly. Afterwards, I ask,
"What do you think of that?" A white-haired man
answers, "In all my life, I've never heard of anything
so beautiful."

September, 1941

Archbishop McDonald appoints me to the staff of
St. Joseph's Seminary. I teach Logic, Latin, Homiletics.
After reading several books on Homiletics, (preaching)
I conclude that the whole course lies in two sentences:
one – have something to say; two – say it. That is my
entire course over a period of four years, once a week.
Many seminarians come for spiritual direction. One of
them arrives one night in a fury. "I'm going to kill him.
I'm going to kill him – the rector, I mean." When he
cools down a bit, I say: "You have a choice between
killing him or becoming a priest. Which do you prefer?"
This seminarain is now the Vicar General of his
diocese.

Edmonton, Alberta, Jasper Avenue – overlooking
the Saskatchewan River Valley and the Munici-
pal Golf Links at 117 St., September, 1942

Father Romeo Ketchen, Pastor of Immaculate
Conception Parish, has asked me to become chaplain
to the young Christian Students' Group. I have
attended several meetings. I feel increasingly

uncomfortable. These girls are taking their religion
seriously. They want to be Christians. They want to
become saints. They want to be apostles.

Over several years, I discover among young people
a burning desire to love God and serve their
neighbour. It is a great joy to see the Holy Spirit so
much alive and at work in so many, many people. A
good number are connected with the Young Christian
Workers, students, farmers, families, etc. As I overlook
the river, it is clear that now I have to make a choice –
either to live a cushy, bourgeois life, or to take God
seriously.

A priest is a witness to the power of God in people.
He brings their love to God and God's love to them.
Slowly, I discover that a priest has the power to bless,
to expel evil, to heal – most of all, to forgive sin; most
of all, to worship the Father through the Son, in the
Holy Spirit; to bring His power to each person, to the
90 billion who constitute the human race in this world
or in the next – to everything, to all creation, the
whole universe at every Mass.

Since 1955, I have been intimately associated with
Catherine Doherty, Father John T. Callahan, Eddie
Doherty, Father Eugene Cullinane and the many
laymen and women and priests who form the Lay
Apostolate of Madonna House. A new civilization is in
the making here, based on essential truths. God loves
me passionately. I can love Him back passionately. I
can lay down my life for others by humble service, day
after day. The white martyrdom is lived out here –
joyfully, relentlessly. The battle between good and evil
is sometimes fierce; always present. In this battle,
priestly spiritual power is eminent.

Priests need a lot of prayer. They need to be
sustained by victim souls, people who unite their
prayer and suffering with the infinite merits of the
Lord Jesus Christ. As I prostrate myself before God in

thanksgiving and adoration; as I thank Our Lady for her presence and constant care, I also remember, with unspeakable gratitude, the hundreds of generous people – priests, nuns, laymen, laywomen who have sustained the priesthood of Jesus Christ in me by their love, their fidelity, their faith, their hope, their prayer. May the blessing of Almighty God – the Father, the Son and the Holy Spirit descend upon them, and upon anyone and everyone who has done me good, upon my enemies, upon those I may have harmed, upon the whole of the human race, upon the whole of creation – and remain forever and ever. Amen.

Other books available through Madonna House
Publications:

by Fr. Emile Brière:
I Met the Humbled Christ in Russia
Katia – A Personal Vision of Catherine Doherty

by Catherine de Hueck Doherty:
Dearly Beloved vol 1&2
Dear Father
Dear Seminarian
Fragments of My Life
The Gospel without Compromise
My Russian Yesterdays
Not without Parables
Our Lady's Unknown Mysteries
Poustinia
Soul of My Soul
and many others

by Fr. Eddie Doherty:
Gall and Honey
Cricket in my Heart
Tumbleweed
Splendour of Sorrow

by Fr. Bob Wild:
His Face Shone Like the Sun
Journey to the Lonely Christ
Love, Love, Love

Catalogue supplied on request.

Madonna House Publications
Combermere, Ontario
K0J 1L0